REMARKABLE
WOMEN
of
NEBRASKA

REMARKABLE
WOMEN
of
NEBRASKA

Andrea M. Riley

THE
History
PRESS

Published by The History Press
An imprint of Arcadia Publishing
Charleston, SC
www.historypress.com

Copyright © 2025 by Andrea M. Riley
All rights reserved

First published 2025

Manufactured in the United States

ISBN 9781467158534

Library of Congress Control Number: 2024951969

For my daughters
Tessa and Eva

CONTENTS

INTRODUCTION

I wasn't sure what I was going to find when I started researching this book. Growing up in Nebraska, I knew about some of the women who had made a historical impact on the state. You can't get through high school here without reading Willa Cather's *My Ántonia*. Mari Sandoz's work was part of the curriculum for my major in Great Plains Studies at the University of Nebraska–Lincoln. I read Bess Streeter Aldrich in my youth, but only remembered her recently when my daughter and her grandmother were reading *A Lantern in Her Hand*. Surprisingly, I had not encountered many of the women in this book until I started looking for them.

Women have played a significant role in Nebraska's history, whether as homesteaders, activists, journalists, educators, artists, writers, philanthropists, entrepreneurs or often a combination of these roles. This book focuses on women in Nebraska's past who had a positive effect on the state. Some were born here or came to live here later in their life. There are many other women not mentioned in this book who came from Nebraska but made their mark in other places, such as Grace Abbott, another Nebraska Hall of Fame member famous for her social work in Chicago. I wanted to focus on women whose accomplishments directly affected Nebraska. There are also many women who are currently doing remarkable things in this state, but that is a book someone else will have to write.

Working on this book reminded me of the Nebraska women in my family history. Unfortunately, I never knew them except through family stories. My great-grandmother Verna McEuen Pugsley was born in Iowa but moved to Nebraska in the early 1900s. Photographs present her as a vivacious and glamorous woman. She lived in both Beatrice and Lincoln and performed in local plays and concerts. My great-grandmother Minnie Dailey Verley was also born in Iowa but moved with her family to homestead in Holt County, Nebraska, in 1904. She and her husband, Benjamin, were likely homesteaders in Garfield County. Verona Verley Pugsley, my grandmother, was born in the Nebraska Sandhills in 1908. She later moved to Lincoln and became a nurse, which was how she met my grandfather. She instilled a strong sense of service in her two children. While the women in my family may not have achievements as great as the women discussed in this book, their lives are also part of Nebraska's history.

I want to thank the many authors who wrote about Nebraska's women before me, which made my job easier. I'd also like to thank History Nebraska and the Bennet Martin Library Heritage Room for their help in accessing historical records and staff at the Office of the Capitol Commission for providing access to take photographs at the state capitol. Special thanks also go to Nikolyn McDonald for taking photographs and my cousin Cilinda Meyer-Scheideler for letting me use her photographs from the Sandhills. Thank you also to my girls for letting me drag them around Omaha and teach them about the Nebraska women who came before them.

Andrea Riley
August 2024

1

HOMESTEADERS

ELIZABETH SCOTT AND ALICE FISH

The Homestead Act was a pivotal piece of legislation the United States Congress passed in 1862. It made it possible for a head of household—whether a man or woman—to claim 160 acres of public land in the western states and territories for a small fee and the effort of "proving up" their claim. This act, along with the Preemption Act of 1841 and the Timber Culture Act of 1873, created a massive migration of settlers to the West, including Nebraska, where Daniel Freemen filed the first homestead claim in 1863. The Kincaid Act of 1904 further encouraged landownership in the Nebraska Sandhills region by allowing for larger land claims. These acts are especially significant in women's history because they allowed single, divorced and widowed women to own land and gain economic independence in an era when such opportunities were scarce. Contrary to the stereotype of the male-dominated frontier, many women—such as Elizabeth Scott and Alice Fish—played crucial roles in setting up and supporting homesteads, transforming the American West and challenging traditional gender roles.

Women were often essential to the success of a homestead, so much so that some men would not even try to homestead without a wife. Women transformed basic, often crude, shelters into homes. In Nebraska, this often took the form of a dugout or "soddy," a house made of bricks of dried sod. Women also managed a large amount of the work required to keep a household running, including cooking, cleaning, sewing, hauling water, preserving meat and other foods, and the daylong tasks of baking and laundry. On top of their household chores, women also had outdoor tasks such as collecting eggs, milking cows and growing a vegetable garden. They even sometimes had to lend a hand with the farmwork.[1]

While history has sometimes depicted women homesteaders as reluctant followers of their fathers or husbands, that was rarely the case. So many single women filed for homesteads under the Kincaid Act that they became a national stereotype. Mari Sandoz (chapter 9), a Nebraska writer and Sandhills native, termed these women "Boston Old Maids" and "Chicago widows."[2] Many homesteader wives were as eager as their husbands to own a home and land of their own. Single women also saw the Homestead Act as an economic opportunity and means to live independently. Homesteading allowed women to challenge Victorian mores and traditional gender roles, but more importantly, it gave women a chance at self-determination in an age when there were few other opportunities for economic independence. In many parts of the West, 10 to 12 percent of successful homesteaders were single women.[3]

Many of these women were widows, including the first documented woman homesteader, Mary Meyer. Meyer was a German immigrant who squatted on property near Beatrice, Nebraska, in 1860 with her husband. While Daniel Freemen filed the first homestead claim on January 1, 1863, his neighbor, Mary, now a widow, filed a claim less than three weeks later. After five years, Mary successfully met the requirements to keep the land. She had built a sixteen-by-twenty-six-foot house, a well, a corral, a chicken coop and a corn crib and cultivated thirty-five acres, fruit trees and grapevines. She later sold her farm in 1877.[4]

Other women homesteaded with their husbands but found themselves in the unenviable position of a widow homesteader when their husband died. While some widows sold their husband's claims and moved back to their families, others stuck it out. Margaret Ann Woodward Canaday started out as a homestead wife but became one of the many women who proved up their claim after their husband's death. She is also recognized as one of the first women in the United States to receive a homestead certificate upon the completion of proving up her claim. Margaret married Riley Canaday in Richland, Iowa, in 1847, and ten years later they traveled by covered wagon to Nebraska Territory. They first settled on land near Nebraska City, where they lived for eight years, struggling against grasshoppers, drought and the weather. They lost their first farm to foreclosure and in 1865 homesteaded in Cass County, near the town of Weeping Water. Four years later, her husband died from typhoid, leaving her with a large family to support. She stayed on her homestead and received title on July 1, 1870. She lived there, raising her children and four grandchildren, for the next thirty years.[5]

Young, unmarried women could claim a homestead if they were willing to put off marriage until the claim was proved up. These women were often motivated by economic necessity, or they took out claims to enlarge their family's property. The latter were often second-generation homesteaders who used the Homestead and other land acts to add property to a family farm or ranch. Once they had proved their claim, they would sell the land to a father or brother. Ella Bohy was such a homesteader. Her father, Gustave Bohy, a French immigrant, homesteaded in Nebraska in 1888. He continued to expand his property with a timber culture claim in 1889 and by buying adjacent land from his neighbor. As soon as Ella was of age, she filed a homestead claim for eighty acres next to her father's property. She proved up the claim, married and sold the land to her father in 1913.[6]

The Chrisman sisters in the Goheen Valley of Custer County, Nebraska, are another example of the practice of taking out claims to expand family property. Their father, Joseph Chrisman, was a rancher who worried that the influx of homesteaders coming into the Sandhills would limit the land available for his ranching operation. As each of his daughters came of age, he had them file claims under the three land acts available at the time—the Homestead Act, the Timber Culture Act and the Preemption Act. Between 1887 and 1892, three of the four girls—Elizabeth, Harriet and Lutie—each acquired 480 acres under these acts. By the time the fourth daughter, Jenny Ruth, came of age, there was no more land available to claim.[7]

For many single women, however, homesteading was a means of achieving economic self-sufficiency. A homestead meant security and an alternative to relying on the charity of their family or working for low wages. As homesteaders, young women could live rent-free in their own home while living off the proceeds of their farm or ranch. While they had to delay marriage while they proved their claim, a homestead could also provide a nice nest egg for the future. Most women didn't work the land themselves, instead hiring farm or ranch hands to work for them. Others leased their land to others to farm. Once they received the title, they would sell or continue to lease.[8]

Two women homesteaders, ELIZABETH SCOTT (1864–1938) and ALICE FISH (1873–1937), serve as examples of the female homesteading experience, although in some ways their experience was unique. Scott and Fish were successful homesteaders and entrepreneurs in Blaine County, Nebraska, during the late nineteenth and early twentieth centuries. They both helped expand their family's property by homesteading but also later homesteaded to support themselves. While a young unmarried woman might file a homestead claim, she usually didn't remain unmarried after proving it up. These two ladies, however, pushed the traditional gender norms of their day by pursuing lives independent of men.

Elizabeth "Libbie" Scott was born in Morton, Illinois. At the age of twenty, she came to Nebraska with her parents. Her father was the leader of a group of immigrants from Illinois that included Libbie's elder sister, her sister's husband and another family. The three families filed homestead claims next to one another in Blaine County, Nebraska. Alice "Allie" Fish was born in Colfax, Iowa. Her family migrated to Nebraska in the late 1870s, settling first at North Loup and then homesteading in Blaine County two miles east of the Scotts in 1889. After building a house and establishing a farm on their new homestead, Allie's parents and sister returned to North Loup, leaving the new homestead in her care. Allie was boarding with the Scotts and running the family homestead, now proved up and deeded in her name, as late as 1897 when the *Brewster News* commented, "Miss Allie Fish is hauling shelled corn from Edith Valley to the Brewster market. She is a plucky young maid determined in her ways, but masculine assistance is thankfully received when it comes to upending a two-bushel bag full of good sound shelled corn."[9]

During the late 1890s, both Allie and Libbie made attempts to follow traditional paths for women of their time. In 1898, Allie sold her personal property and announced she was moving to Ord, Nebraska, nearer to her parents, to open a millinery shop. That summer, Libbie surprised everyone by suddenly marrying her cousin, William Hughes "Hugh" Scott. More surprising was the age difference between the bride and groom: Libbie was thirty-three, and her new husband was only fifteen. The new couple's union did not last long. Although they weren't officially divorced until 1905, a newspaper article at the time indicated that Libbie had deserted Hugh only two weeks after the wedding. She went back to live with her parents. Allie too was soon back in Blaine County, living with the Scotts as well. Each had failed in her attempt at fulfilling the cultural norms of the day. Between 1898 and 1902, they redefined themselves, beginning their lifelong domestic partnership and gaining the respect of their community, despite pursuing a course of life different from most women.[10]

In 1902, Libbie and Allie explained how their partnership came about in an article for the *Omaha World-Herald*. They said:

(RECORD OF PATENTS.)   PATENT NUMBER   **120622**

4-404-tyr.

The United States of America,

To all to whom these presents shall come, Greeting:

Broken Bow 01540.

WHEREAS, There has been deposited in the GENERAL LAND OFFICE of the United States a Certificate of the Register of the Land Office at Broken Bow, Nebraska, whereby it appears that, pursuant to the Act of Congress approved 20th May, 1862, "To secure Homesteads to Actual Settlers on the Public Domain," and the acts supplemental thereto, the claim of

ALLIE S. FISH

has been established and duly consummated, in conformity to law, for the northeast quarter of Section thirty-two in Township twenty-two north of Range twenty-one west of the Sixth Principal Meridian, Nebraska, containing one hundred sixty acres,

according to the Official Plat of the Survey of the said Land, returned to the GENERAL LAND OFFICE by the Surveyor General:

NOW KNOW YE, That there is, therefore, granted by the UNITED STATES unto the said Allie S. Fish the tract of Land above described; TO HAVE AND TO HOLD the said tract of Land, with the appurtenances thereof, unto the said Allie S. Fish

and to   her   heirs and assigns forever.

IN TESTIMONY WHEREOF, I,   William H. Taft   , President of the United States of America, have caused these letters to be made Patent, and the seal of the General Land Office to be hereunto affixed.

(SEAL)   GIVEN under my hand, at the City of Washington, the TWENTY-FOURTH   day of MARCH   , in the year of our Lord one thousand nine hundred and   TEN, and of the Independence of the United States the one hundred and THIRTY-FOURTH.

By the President: Wm. H. Taft

By   M. P. Le Ray   , Secretary.

Recorder of the General Land Office.

Allie Fish's land patent. *Bureau of Land Management (BLM), General Land Office (GLO) Records Automation website.*

After carefully thinking the matter over we both came to the conclusion that we could make a better living for ourselves in raising cattle and operating a ranch that in any vocation presenting itself to us in this whole western country. Women had made a success of many things that men supposed they could know nothing about, and we didn't see why we couldn't succeed as ranchers. Both of us had taught in the public schools, and there was nothing to that field to make us as independent as we wished.[11]

According to that same article, they "secured a half section of Nebraska land, and in 1900 added to their possessions two homesteads where they proceeded to build up a successful stock business which now makes them independent." The original section of land came from 160 acres Libbie's father deeded to her and the 160 acres Allie already had from her father's homestead. In the first two years, they raised 400 head of cattle, cut and stacked 100 tons of hay and cultivated 80 acres of corn. They also installed a gasoline engine pump to water their cattle and fencing on eight pastures.[12]

Neither of the women were strangers to running a farm. Allie had proven herself by running the Fish family homestead on her own for several years. Libbie also had experience running her own operation. As her father told a local Illinois newspaper, he had turned over half his operation to Libbie a few years prior, as she "had previously demonstrated her ability as a 'cowboy' and ranch manager."[13] Allie and Libbie did most of the work on their ranch but hired men for some of the harder tasks like building fences and breaking sod.[14]

Over time, they continued to improve their ranch, adding larger barns, windmills and in 1904 a six-room frame house. Prior to that they lived in a soddy that Libbie's parents had built. They raised a variety of animals besides cattle, including hogs, chickens, mules and horses. They grew speltz and rye as well as corn and hay.[15] Allie and Libbie were happy with the life they had made for themselves and professed the benefits of being women ranchers in a 1902 article:

Ranch life is a most agreeable one for the active young woman who has her own way in the world to make. And we are not sure but that it beats a life of elegant leisure in every particular, while we are sure it does in some respects. We do not consider ranch life as difficult, or wearing, as the labor of the wife, cook or housekeeper, or clerking behind a counter, or in an occupation where you are on our feed from morning until evening.[16]

They wrapped the article up noting, "Taking it all in all we consider it the most free and easy as well as the most profitable occupation women can find."[17]

Besides being successful ranchers, Libbie and Allie were active in charities helping women and children. They served as officers in the Blaine County chapter of Homes for the Friendless, an organization that placed children born out of wedlock with foster parents and ran a home for unwed mothers in the state's capital, Lincoln. The ladies actively supported their local schools and teachers by donating educational materials, organizing school activities, and renting homes to teachers. Allie often took part in fundraising events for the schools and worked for over a decade to promote construction of a public

Legal Notices.

LAND OFFICE, Broken Bow, NEBR.
Jan. 22nd 1906.

Notice is hereby given that the following-named settler has filed notice of his intention to make final proof in support of his claim, and that said proof will be made before Clerk District Court at Brewster, Neb. on March 16, 1906 viz:

LIBBIE R. SCOTT,

Brewster, Neb., for the se¼ se¼ Sec. 27, ne¼ ne¼ Sec 34, n½ nw¼ 35, Tp. 22 N. R. 21 W.

He names the following witnesses to prove his continuous residence upon and cultivation of said land, viz:

William M. Scott, Charles E. Van Neste, Charles J. Fletcher, Hugh R. Ferguson all of Brewster, Nebraska.

1-26-3-2   JAMES WHITEHEAD,
Register,

Legal notice of Libbie Scott's homestead claim. *From* The Brewster (NE) News, *March 2, 1906.*

auditorium in Brewster, the closest town to their ranch. They were also active in the Brewster Chautauqua committee, an educational and social group that sponsored events in the community. Libbie chaired the Children's Activities committee between 1920 and 1928 while Allie served as treasurer and fundraising chair.[18]

Allie and Libbie were also politically active. Between 1908 and 1913, they contributed to a weekly column in the *Brewster News*. The column covered the comings and goings of residents in the Edith Valley area where they lived, but they also used the column to discuss women's rights and political issues. By 1910, women in Nebraska who owned land or had children could vote on school elections, but it was still controversial that they could vote at all. The Blaine County ballot that year included a question about creating a county high school. The Scott-Fish ranch house was the polling place for Edith Valley, so they had a front row seat for the election. Their August 26 column observed, "The election in Edith precinct passed very quietly despite the predictions of Anti-Suffragists that women at the polls would certainly bring out the very worst that is in man. We do not share these opinions however so please give us a chance to demonstrate." Later in November, after the general election, they wrote, "The election this year was especially interesting on account of the women having a chance to vote, and they seem to enjoy the new experience."[19]

Libbie continued to support women's suffrage. She was an officer of the Blaine County Federated Women's Club and was active in the suffrage debate in 1914. The group had remarkable success in a vote to amend the state constitution to allow women to vote. Even though the measure failed at the state level, Blaine County voted to support it, 196 to 144. Meanwhile, Allie was active on local school boards, school bond committees and the Blaine County Republican Party. In 1913, she made the fifty-mile trip to Sargent, Nebraska, to hear William Jennings Bryan speak. In 1922, she was the Blaine County delegate to the Republican Party state convention and was a voting member on the Blaine County Republican Central Committee many times.[20]

In 1912, Libbie and Allie, aged forty-eight and thirty-nine, decided to move to town. They sold off their farm equipment and stock, rented out part of their land and brought in a Scott family member to run their ranch. After a well-deserved vacation to New Orleans and Illinois, they set up a household in Brewster and bought Libbie's brother-in-law's dry goods store from her sister, whose husband had recently passed away. Allie oversaw the day-to-day management of the store while Libbie took care of their home. The store sold dry goods and clothing, but the ladies also bought and sold locally produced food items and furs. At one point, their store included a state-licensed cream station where local cream, butter and eggs were sold or traded.[21]

Their business in Brewster fared well in the booming World War I economy. They bought seventy-nine acres of land at the edge of Brewster and built a new house and barn in 1915. A few years later, they added rental cottages to their property. In 1922, they won the mail contract between Brewster and the rail line at Dunning. This allowed them to start a new line of business: freighting, first by wagon and later by trucks. The ladies brought many other innovations to Brewster, including installation of the first gasoline pump in 1923, a ladies' hair salon in 1924 and a light plant that provided electricity to their home and rental cottages in 1925.[22]

Libbie Scott and Allie Fish were mainstays of the community in Brewster for many years. Even the hardships of the Great Depression couldn't get them down. The 1930s brought a general economic downturn in the Sandhills and the failure of the Brewster bank. Scott and Fish also lost income due to competition from the Farmers Union Cooperative and the loss of the mail contract. But they didn't give up. When faced with an announcement from the Farmers Union that they planned to open a grocery store, Libbie and Allie went all in. They mortgaged their remaining property for a loan of $6,000 to remodel their existing store and add on a building next door for an International Harvester dealership. Their act of faith resulted in a small boom in Brewster as other businesses in town remodeled and repainted. While the boom didn't overcome the difficulties of the Great Depression, Allie and Libbie still managed to keep their store open.[23]

Neither Allie nor Libbie lived to see the end of that difficult period in U.S. history. One morning in February 1937, Allie collapsed on her way to the store. She died several hours later, having suffered a heart attack. Allie left everything to Libbie in her will, but it turned out that it was not much. The ranch operation could not pay its debts, and the store was losing money. Libbie tried to carry on, but in November 1937, she sold the store. Later that year, she fell ill and sold her house in Brewster to move in with her nephew and his wife in Anselmo, Nebraska, where she died in January 1938.[24]

Despite the financial losses at the end of their lives, Allie Fish and Libbie Scott accomplished remarkable things. They both worked farms for their families as young women, successfully proved up their own homesteads and ran a dry goods store, post office and freighting company for many years. They were innovators and economic mainstays in their community. They also took part in civic organizations that supported the welfare of women, children and local schools. Both ladies were highly respected in their community. People remembered Allie as a "landmark in the community" and "a booster for any community enterprise." Members of the community noted how Libbie was "always [extending] a helping hand to those about her, specially the children and young people." Allie and Libbie serve as examples of what women homesteaders could do. While their story may not be typical of women homesteaders, their persistence, faith and boosterism certainly reflect the spirit of all the women who looked to turn the Nebraska prairie into their home.[25]

2

CRUSADERS

ANNA WOODBEY, ADA BITTENBENDER AND CLARA COLBY

The temperance and suffrage movements in Nebraska were closely connected during the late nineteenth and early twentieth centuries. Women's suffrage gained momentum partly because of its association with temperance. As women's rights activist Susan B. Anthony noted, "The only hope of the Anti-Saloon League's success lies in putting the ballot into the hands of women."[26] Key figures such as Anna Woodbey, Ada Bittenbender and Clara Bewick Colby made significant contributions to these movements in Nebraska. While these women faced many challenges—from societal opposition to internal disagreements within the movements—in the end, their stories illustrate the determination and resilience of women crusaders to bring about reform in the state.

Nebraska's history with temperance began in 1855 with a law prohibiting the manufacture and sale of intoxicating liquors, that the population largely ignored. By 1858, a licensing system had replaced outright prohibition. Twelve years later, in 1870, the first temperance organization in Nebraska, the Independent Order of Good Templars, resolved to repeal the licensing law and prohibit the sale of alcohol. Petitioners and legislators tried to enact temperance laws throughout the 1870s and 1880s, with no success.[27]

Women played a significant role in the temperance crusade. Temperance, rather than suffrage, was the social and political cause of many nineteenth-century women because of the large amounts of alcohol most men drank. A drunkard for a husband could result in abuse, homelessness, abandonment or loss of financial security because of poor business decisions or inability to hold down a job. Prohibition wasn't just a moral cause for women of the time but an attempt to obtain protection under the law.[28]

In 1873, temperance activist Carrie Nation visited the Lincoln Woman's Christian Temperance Union (WCTU) and emboldened the women of in the state's capital to take direct action against local saloons. Women started entering saloons in the hundreds to pray. This led to ordinances prohibiting women from congregating on the streets or entering saloons in pairs. Foiled in their efforts, the Lincoln crusaders turned to the organization of a young men's reading room, which eventually became a local library. They also laid the foundation for many of Lincoln's charitable foundations.[29]

In 1874, temperance activists formed a state Prohibition Party and offered candidates for governor and other offices. Several women candidates ran for office, including F. Bernice Kennedy, who ran for superintendent of public instruction, and Mrs. C.M. Woodward, who ran for Congress. One of the party's more notable candidates, however, was Anna Woodbey (1855–1901), an African American minister and orator. Woodbey was a notable speaker on temperance, suffrage and prohibition from an early age. Even as a child, she gave speeches before large groups, advocating for prohibition. Born Annie Goodwin in Harrisburg, Pennsylvania, and raised in Canada and Michigan, she married George Washington Woodbey in Kansas in 1873. They had three children and moved to Omaha around 1882. Woodbey was active in religious and reformist circles, including the Woman's Home and Foreign Missionary Society and the Negro Woman's Club of Omaha. She and her husband were both Baptist ministers, and she often filled his place behind the pulpit during his absences. Woodbey used her oratory skills to advance the causes of temperance and women's suffrage and became known around the state as "the distinguished lady orator of Omaha."[30]

Woodbey also was the only African American member of the Woman's Christian Temperance Union and served as her local chapter's president and delegate to several state conventions. In Nebraska, the WCTU formed in 1875 when Ada Bittenbender and Hattie B. Slaughter brought all the local unions together for a meeting in Lincoln to create a state organization. The state organization hoped to promote total abstinence and suppress the liquor trade. It developed over the years to include broader temperance efforts. Despite some successes in electing temperance representatives in the 1870s and achieving local restrictions, statewide prohibition efforts initially failed.[31]

Woodbey's visibility in the prohibition movement and her oratory skills made her a contender for public office, and the Prohibition Party nominated her as their candidate for regent of the University of Nebraska in 1895. It was significant that they did so given her race. The prohibition newspaper *Our Nation's Anchor* (Lincoln) reported, "Mrs. Woodbey is, we think, the first Negro woman ever honored with a nomination on a state ticket by any political party in the United States."[32] Although the Prohibition Party in 1895 was too outnumbered to get any of their candidates elected, Woodbey remained active in the party, serving as an alternate delegate to the party's state convention in 1896. She died in 1901, but the temperance movement persisted in Nebraska, contributing to statewide prohibition in 1914 and the passage of national Prohibition in 1918.[33]

BESIDES HELPING ORGANIZE THE state's WCTU, ADA BITTENBENDER (1848–1925) made significant contributions to the suffrage movement, women's rights, the temperance movement and legislative reforms in Nebraska during the late nineteenth and early twentieth centuries. She was also one of Nebraska's first women attorneys. Born in Macedonia, Pennsylvania, she attended the Binghamton, New York commercial college, graduating in 1869. She then received her teaching qualifications at the Pennsylvania State Normal School at Bloomsburg. In 1878, she married attorney Henry Clay Bittenbender of Bloomsburg, Pennsylvania, and later that year they moved to Osceola, Nebraska. Bittenbender taught school while her husband established his law firm. A year later, her husband bought the local newspaper, *The Record*. The Bittenbenders were both temperance advocates and used the paper as an outlet for their cause. Ada became an editor of her husband's paper and, as one biographer said, "made it an able, fearless, moral, family and temperance newspaper."[34]

Bittenbender participated in the formation of the Nebraska Woman Suffrage Association in 1881. Although neighboring states such as Wyoming and Colorado gave women the vote during the second half the nineteenth century, women's suffrage was slow to come to Nebraska. The legislature brought the matter before the Nebraska electorate three times, in 1871, 1882 and 1914, but each time it failed.[35]

The Nebraska woman's suffrage movement can trace its origins to Amelia Bloomer's 1855 message before the Nebraska Territorial Legislature. Bloomer, a temperance and suffrage activist from Council Bluffs, Iowa, persuaded lawmakers in both legislative houses to consider a woman's suffrage bill, but the legislature didn't add the measure to the agenda until the last day of the session, when it was too late for a vote. Instead of Nebraska becoming the first state to give women the vote, the new state constitution in 1855 specifically denied women suffrage. The state movement lay dormant until 1870, when eastern women's rights advocates, including Susan B. Anthony, visited Nebraska to organize local support for a challenge to the state constitution. The 1871 state constitutional convention considered women's suffrage, but the amendment failed by four to one when it went before male voters.[36]

Part of the reason for the 1871 defeat was a pro-suffrage speaker's claim that if women got the vote, liquor would be banned in the state within six months. This claim, along with the fact that the suffrage movement grew out of the temperance movement, put the two issues together in voters' minds. It took another eight years for the suffrage movement to recover in Nebraska. Activist Erasmus Cornell, publisher of the *Western Women's Journal* in Lincoln, invited Susan B. Anthony to speak in Nebraska again in 1879. The day of her speech, Stanton and Cornell organized fifteen supporters into the first lasting suffrage organization in the state, the Thayer County Woman Suffrage Association. By the end of 1881, when the state association formed, there were thirty-nine women suffrage associations active in Nebraska.[37]

The members of the Nebraska Woman Suffrage Association elected Ada Bittenbender as their recording secretary during their first election. Their first order of business was to secure the submission of a woman suffrage amendment to the state constitution. Bittenbender was one of three campaign speakers for the suffrage amendment and served as chairperson of the state campaign committee for its last three months. At the annual convention in 1881, she took to the stage to outline the campaign for the constitutional amendment vote in 1882. At the following annual meeting, she was elected president of the association.[38]

In 1882, not only was Bittenbender the president of the Nebraska suffrage association, but she was also a newly minted attorney. She was the first woman in the state to pass the bar. Later in 1888, she became the third woman to be allowed to practice before the U.S. Supreme Court. She would later serve as the national Woman's Christian Temperance Union attorney and won cases against saloons and for the rights of women and children.[39]

Unfortunately, the campaign for the state constitutional amendment in 1882 failed yet again—this time, however, by a ratio of two to one. A multitude of issues plagued the effort. Logistically, the Nebraska Woman Suffrage Association lacked enough workers to cover the state. Lack of funds made it difficult to rent venues or pay for advertising. Lack of political support from either party and rifts within the national suffrage movement also played a role. The national suffrage party split over whether to focus on amending state constitutions or to seek a national Constitutional amendment. The temperance movement also served as a distraction. After the failed state amendment in Nebraska in 1882, the woman's suffrage movement in the state would remain relatively quiet for nearly thirty years.[40]

With the women's suffrage cause at a dead end in Nebraska, Bittenbender shifted her attention to her work as an attorney and the temperance movement. In these efforts, she found remarkable success. As superintendent of the Department of Legislation and Petitions for the Nebraska WCTU, she aided the passage of multiple bills through the Nebraska state legislature. One of the bills required that students receive instruction in physiology and hygiene with specific reference to the effects of alcohol and drugs on the body. Other bills established an industrial school and a home for penitent women and girls, the latter intended to lessen prostitution. At the request of the Lincoln WCTU, Bittenbender took charge of a tobacco bill that prohibited minors from buying tobacco products and saw it through to passage.[41]

In 1889, Bittenbender and her husband moved to Washington, D.C., and until 1892, she worked for the National WCTU. One of her accomplishments during this time was to write the *National Prohibitory Amendment Guide*, a manual to aid local WCTU organizations in their work toward a Prohibition amendment to the Constitution. She was also active in supporting bills and petitions before Congress. She drafted a bill for the protection of women, offered in Congress by Senator Henry W. Blair of New Hampshire. Her work to make the bill compatible with existing law helped it pass. It also resulted in Blair supporting her admission to practice before the U.S. Supreme Court in 1888.[42]

In 1891, she ran for Nebraska Supreme Court judge on the Prohibition Party ticket, receiving nearly 5 percent of the vote. This was not only a significant achievement for a woman at the time, but it was also the largest vote in proportion ever given to a Prohibition Party candidate. Bittenbender continued to work for the Nebraska WCTU after her return to Nebraska. She eventually gave up the practice of law and devoted her time to philosophical studies. Ada Bittenbender passed away in Lincoln at the age of seventy-seven in 1925, having retired from public life following her husband's death. She was one of the few early Nebraska temperance and suffrage activists to live long enough to see the fruition of their decades of work. Congress ratified

REMARKABLE WOMEN OF NEBRASKA

the Eighteenth Amendment prohibiting the manufacture, sale and transport of alcohol in 1919 and the Nineteenth Amendment, giving women the right to vote, in 1920.[43]

AFTER THE SECOND ATTEMPT to give women the right to vote in Nebraska failed in 1882, a few diehard suffragists kept the movement alive through newspapers like the *Hebron Journal* and the *Woman's Tribune*.[44] The most instrumental advocate for woman's suffrage in Nebraska during this time was CLARA BEWICK COLBY (1846–1916). Praising Colby's efforts, Susan B. Anthony said that "if we could all work as Mrs. Colby does, our cause would move on." A contemporary biographical sketch described Colby as "Nebraska's most prominent suffragist."[45]

Clara Bewick was born in England and moved with her family to Wisconsin when she was eight years old. She graduated from the University of Wisconsin in 1869 and taught history and Latin before marrying Leonard Wright Colby, an attorney. Her passion for equal rights was evident early in her career when she resigned her position at the university in protest over equal pay. The couple moved to Beatrice, Nebraska, in 1872, where their family grew. In 1885, they adopted a boy, Clarence, from an orphan train. In 1891, Leonard was present on the Pine Ridge Indian Reservation at the time of the massacre at Wounded Knee and returned home with a baby girl, Zintkala Nuni (Lost Bird).[46]

Clara Colby honed her activism while in Beatrice. She was a member of the Ladies Library Association of Beatrice and helped form the first public library in that town. Libraries were often associated with the temperance movement as an alternative to men gathering in saloons; however, the motive of the Ladies Library Association was community improvement. The Colbys provided space for the library in Leonard Colby's law offices. Given the library's location, it made sense that Clara became its first librarian. The library enterprise met with opposition from the local community and fierce competition with the Red Ribbon temperance movement, which had its own reading room in town. Despite the eventual failure of the project because of competition and lack of funding, Colby later donated the library's collection to the WTCU for their library. This library eventually became the Public Library of Beatrice.[47]

The tenacity Colby showed in trying to preserve the library in Beatrice served her well in efforts to keep the Nebraska Woman Suffrage Association alive. She was a founder of the group, along with Ada Bittenbender, in 1881.

After the amendment failure in 1882, Colby agreed to publish a suffrage journal, and in August 1883, she made good on her promise by publishing the first edition of the new suffrage newspaper, the *Woman's Tribune*. That same year she spoke before the Nebraska legislature, assuring them that the suffrage movement was alive and well in the state and that she believed that they would one day prevail. Colby's dedication to the cause of suffrage was so strong that when the association had to suspend financial support for the *Woman's Tribune* a year later, she single-handedly kept it in print. This likely led to her election as president of the suffrage association in 1885, a position she held until 1889 and honorarily until 1898.[48]

The *Woman's Tribune* turned Colby into a national leader. In 1889, it became the newspaper of the National Woman Suffrage Association. It provided news about major suffragist meetings, legislative developments and speeches from the movement, spreading information to isolated women throughout the West. She ran the paper for twenty-six years while advocating around the country for women's suffrage. Her paper was the second-longest-running newspaper of any movement and the longest paper to run without national support. Colby published the paper until 1909, moving it first to Washington, D.C., in 1889, when her husband became assistant attorney general of the United States and then later to Portland, Oregon, in 1904, when she moved there to further the cause of women's suffrage on the Pacific coast.[49]

After moving to Washington, D.C., Colby's involvement in the suffrage movement was more at the national and international level. During 1910–11, she returned to her English homeland to support the suffrage movement there. She was a delegate to various national and international suffrage groups in the 1900s and 1910s, including meetings of the International Woman Suffrage Alliance in Amsterdam and Budapest and the International Peace Congress in London and the Hague. She also spoke and lectured around the United States, addressing legislatures in Nebraska, Missouri, Michigan and Rhode Island about women's suffrage. Besides these activities, she also contributed the chapter "History of Woman's Suffrage in Nebraska" for the *History of Woman's Suffrage* written by Elizabeth Cady Stanton and Susan B. Anthony. She died in 1916, not yet having won the right to vote.[50]

Although Clara Colby left Nebraska in 1889, she left the state's suffrage movement with the impetus to continue their fight. In the mid-1910s, the suffrage movement in Nebraska entered its third serious attempt to pass a state suffrage bill. By 1914, many of the states around Nebraska had given women the right to vote. Once again, it took a visit from the National American Woman Suffrage Association to urge the state association into action. The anti-suffrage movement in Nebraska was quite fierce, however. By the mid-1910s, half of Nebraska's population was foreign-born. These

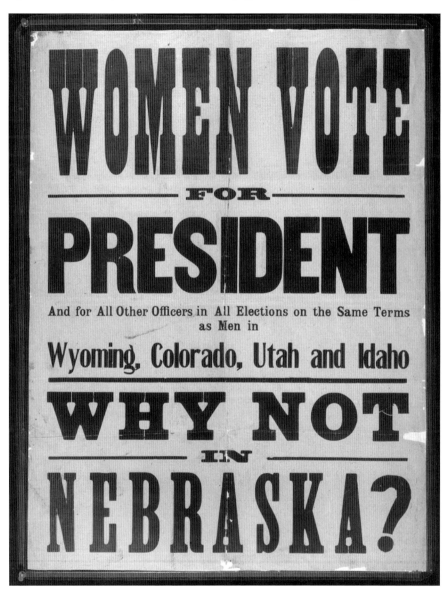

Color transparency of a poster, "Women Vote For President." *Nebraska State Historical Society Photograph Collections.*

immigrant groups were unfamiliar with women taking part in government. Many immigrants were unwilling to give women a say even in family decisions. Meanwhile, the suffrage movement's ties to the temperance movement still concerned many anti-suffragists. Saloons, alcohol manufacturers and suppliers worried that giving women the vote would lead to prohibition. They feared prohibition would affect the state's economy given that grain was used to produce alcohol. Despite this opposition, the state movement brought a suffrage amendment to a vote in 1914 with help from the national movement. Yet again the measure failed, but this time the margin was much less, with ten to nine against.[51]

After the 1914 defeat, the state suffrage association expected a four-year wait before they could try again, but the state legislature surprised them by passing a limited suffrage bill in 1917. This law allowed women to vote in municipal elections and for presidential electors. It was the most that could be done without an amendment to the state's constitution. The suffragists had met with success, but the battle for a woman's right to vote was not over in the state. Anti-suffragists petitioned to have the law put to a referendum. They collected the required thirty thousand signatures to block the law from going into effect. The Nebraska Woman Suffrage Association responded with an investigation of the signatures. By early 1918, they had compiled evidence of rampant fraud and sued to stop the state from continuing the referendum petition. Evidence included signatures of minors and deceased persons and addresses that didn't exist. Ironically, it was women in the anti-suffrage movement who had led the petition effort, and it was because of their reluctance to actively participate in politics the petition didn't withstand the scrutiny of the suffragists. The petition process was opened to fraud because anti-suffragist women paid others to collect signatures.[52]

In the end, the efforts of the Nebraska Woman Suffrage Association proved unnecessary. The Nebraska Supreme Court only began to hear arguments on the referendum in June 1919, a month after the House of Representatives passed the Nineteenth Amendment. The state suffrage association was so sure the national woman's suffrage amendment would pass that they had already changed their name to the League of Women Voters. Nevertheless, the Nebraska Supreme Court voted in favor of the suffragists. Sixty-four years after Amelia Bloomer encouraged the territorial legislature to consider giving women in Nebraska the vote, they finally had it.[53]

The intertwined history of the temperance and suffrage movements in Nebraska during the late nineteenth and early twentieth centuries highlights the formidable spirit and resilience of women crusaders. Figures such as Anna Woodbey, Ada Bittenbender and Clara Bewick Colby played crucial roles in these movements, overcoming many challenges to fight for societal reform and women's rights. Their efforts not only contributed to the eventual success of prohibition and women's suffrage but also laid the groundwork for future generations of women to continue advocating for equality and justice. The legacies of these women serve as enduring inspirations, proving that with unwavering determination and collective action, significant societal change is achievable.

3

PHILANTHROPISTS

THE CREIGHTON SISTERS, ANNA WILSON AND SARAH JOSLYN

Philanthropy has long been a cornerstone in the development and enrichment of communities, and Omaha, Nebraska, is no exception. The generosity and vision of remarkable Omaha women such as the Creighton sisters, Anna Wilson and Sarah Joslyn have profoundly influenced the development of the city. Each of these women used their wealth to establish educational institutions and hospitals or to support the arts and other social services. Their unique backgrounds and personal convictions shaped their charitable endeavors and left a mark on Omaha that is still visible today. Their stories provide insight into the powerful role of women in philanthropy and community development in Nebraska's largest city.

MARY LUCRETIA CREIGHTON (1834–1876) and SARAH EMILY CREIGHTON (1840–1888) were born in Dayton, Ohio, to David Wareham, a builder and political leader. Mary Lucretia met Edward Crieghton, a friend of her father, when he was building telegraph lines out of Dayton. He moved west to Omaha in 1856, but he didn't forget the young woman and returned to Ohio to marry her later that year. In 1861, the couple settled in Omaha, where Edward was the general superintendent of the Pacific Telegraph Company. Sarah Emily met Edward's brother, John, while visiting her sister in Omaha, and they married in 1868. Both couples lived together for many years. After losing infant children, the sisters remained childless, leaving them energy and opportunity to pursue interests outside their family. Both sisters and their husbands were devout Catholics and dedicated philanthropists, but each had a distinct personality. Mary Lucretia was the pretty one everyone loved. Sarah Emily was stern, an organizer and a hands-on leader. Mary Lucretia regularly visited Omaha's poorest neighborhoods in the city to distribute the twenty-five dollars a day Edward gave her to share with the needy. Sarah Emily, while equally generous, instead gave large donations to institutions.[54]

Edward Creighton made a substantial fortune building the transcontinental telegraph and founding the First National Bank. He also engaged in cattle ranching and other business enterprises. When he died suddenly in 1874, he left Mary Lucretia his sole heir and the richest widow in Omaha at that time. He also left it to her discretion what to do with their fortune. According to family members, the two sisters were interested in founding an educational institution because their husbands were not well educated. In 1875, Mary Lucretia bequeathed $100,000 (equivalent to $2.3 million today) to start a Catholic college for boys, which led to the founding of Creighton University.[55]

When Mary Lucretia died in 1876, it fell to her sister and brother-in-law to see her dream come to fruition. Creighton University opened in 1878 with free tuition thanks to Mary Lucretia's bequest. Sarah Emily and Edward contributed additional money to the college, making Creighton a science-oriented institution. They financed a chemistry building and an observatory during the 1880s. They also promoted the school's religious identity. Sarah Emily persuaded the Jesuits to build St. John's Church, which became the heart of the campus upon its completion in 1888. She also helped to finance construction of a new wing to the main college building to house the college's growing Jesuit community. Sarah Emily also made significant personal donations to various other institutions around Omaha, including St. Joseph Hospital, St. John's Church and the Poor Clares.[56]

WHILE THE CREIGHTONS WERE early philanthropists of great respectability, making their fortune in the business of westward expansion, ANNA WILSON (1833–1911) was something else altogether. She was known as "Omaha's most famous madam," and her wealth originated from gambling and prostitution in the area known as the "Burnt District" of Omaha. Like Mary Lucretia Creighton, Anna Wilson left a substantial fortune to charity, but unlike Creighton, she was not without considerable controversy.

Little is certain about Anna Wilson's background. There is no year of birth on her grave, but it says she was seventy-eight years old in 1911,

St. John's Church at Creighton University, Omaha, Nebraska. *Author's collection*.

which would make her born in 1833. Reverend Charles W. Savage, a missionary among the women of the Burnt District who eulogized Anna Wilson after her death, claimed that she came from Georgia and was the daughter of a Baptist minister "descended of a long line of aristocratic southerners."[57] She apparently ran away from her grandfather's house in Cairo, Illinois, with an army captain named Wilson. After the captain deserted her, she fell into a life of prostitution. At some point, she moved to New Orleans, where she met Dan Allen, a gambler, who persuaded her to move to Omaha with him in 1867. Anna worked in his gambling house and was his companion and common-law wife for thirteen years until his death in 1884.[58]

Allen left all his money to Wilson, who erected an elaborate monument in the Prospect Hill Cemetery to mark his grave. Two years after Allen's death, she opened a brothel at Ninth and Douglas Streets in Omaha. It was a red brick mansion with bay windows and a porch decorated with columns depicting naked women. It had twenty-five rooms with forty-six beds.[59] By all accounts Anna was good to the women who worked for her. Reverend Savage said, "She never ruined girls….When the unsullied girl appeared before her, she used her purse and influence to turn her into the right path. She has given many a repentant girl a chance to undo her past and start over again."[60] Another person recalled how she sent many women back to their parents or husbands, "telling them it was the last life in the underworld for a woman to lead and that she did not want any woman in her house who was not confirmed to that life."[61] She also paid medical expenses to help prevent the spread of venereal disease, and if one of her girls died by suicide, she paid for the funeral costs. [62] While the situation Anna Wilson and her girls were in was not ideal, she at least tried to do her best for them.

Anna retired in the 1890s and moved to a quiet but palatial home on Wirt Street in Omaha. She lived comfortably off the money from her real estate investments, which made up about half of her fortune. Having no other family, she lived on her own except for a butler, a woman servant, her pet parrot and her two dogs Wilson also used her fortune to give to charity, but it was her charitable acts at the very end of her life that brought the most interest and caused the most controversy.[63]

The first controversy arose when she offered her old brothel to the city to use as an emergency hospital. The city needed another hospital, but many criticized city leaders for even considering the donation. They were especially reproachful because the city was to rent the building from

Wilson until the end of her life. For this reason, at least one critic accused her of trying to take advantage of the city because "property in that district is no longer rentable at the handsome figure of $125 a month." The red-light district had been "dismantled by the law," and "the rent will be a sure accumulation to her splendid blood-bought fortune."[64] Others, however, came to her defense. One person wrote an editorial to the *Omaha Daily News*:

> *I have lived in this city for over forty-eight years and am personally acquainted with Miss Anna Wilson, and will say this in her behalf: That there is a woman (notwithstanding her past life) that it would be well if a lot of our so-called Christian women would take pattern after.*[65]

The writer also noted how Wilson had dissuaded girls from entering prostitution and that she had "given thousands of dollars away in this city for charity."[66] The city did accept the building, which eventually became a venereal disease clinic. Wilson left a note accompanying the deed to the property stating how she hoped that when the property no longer was a good location for a hospital that its sale would allow the city to purchase a new site to construct its emergency hospital.[67]

Around 1910, Anna Wilson suffered a stroke. Acknowledging that the end of her life was near and that her money would end up going to the city anyway, as she had no heirs, her final acts were to determine exactly who her fortune and property would benefit. Her fortune, mostly in real estate, was estimated at anywhere between $200,000 to $500,000, which would be $6 to $16 million today.[68] In her will, she left her home and the residence she owned next to it to the Old People's Home. Wilson was quoted to have said, "Those old ladies will appreciate sitting on the veranda seeing people go by on the boulevard." According to a newspaper article, she had often sent a pound of tea to each of the women in the home and they regarded her as a friend.[69]

After various bequests to hospitals, including the Clarkson Memorial Hospital and the Wise Memorial Hospital, her will split what remained of her fortune between the Creche, Child Saving Institute, Prospect Hill Cemetery Association, Old People's Home, City Mission, Associated Charities and the City of Omaha. One newspaper stated that it believed that all donations would be accepted. "I'm glad there was a sinner good enough to leave us money," Mrs. T.L. Kimball, president of the Creche board, told the paper in discussing Wilson's bequest. Many of the recipient institutions planned to use the money for new or better buildings.[70] According to Anna Wilson's attorney, her last act was to sign a $500 check to the city for remodeling the hospital building she was leaving them, asking that it be called the City Emergency Hospital. She added a note: "In giving this property to the city my sole desire and purpose was to do good to others, not to benefit myself; to help distressed humanity, not to obtain public favor or add credit to my name."[71]

Anna Wilson was buried next to Dan Allen in the Prospect Hill Cemetery. Despite her reputation, her charitable contributions had a significant effect on the city and resulted in her becoming one of the best-known local women of her era. After Anna's death, a prominent Omaha woman annually laid a

Anna Wilson and Dan Allen's grave, Prospect Hill Cemetery, Omaha, Nebraska. *Courtesy of Tessa Riley.*

wreath on her grave in thanks for her many financial contributions around the city. The tradition continues today with the laying of flowers around her grave on Memorial Day.[72]

WHILE THE CREIGHTON SISTERS and Anna Wilson each benefited Omaha in their own ways, the city's most prominent philanthropist was SARAH JOSLYN (1851–1940). Joslyn is renowned for her extensive contributions to cultural and civic institutions in the city, particularly the Joslyn Art Museum, formerly known as the Joslyn Memorial. Her life and work left an indelible mark on Omaha, demonstrating her belief in using wealth for the public good and her commitment to improving her community.

Sarah Hannah Selleck was born in Vermont, where she eventually met and married George Joslyn in 1872. The couple spent a few years in Montreal, Canada, before moving to Omaha in 1880. When the couple arrived in the city, they had little money to their name. They lived in the printing plant where George worked. He had come to Omaha to open a branch office of Iowa Printing called the Omaha Newspaper Union. Sarah managed two hotels while her husband built up his business, buying up stock so that he eventually owned the company and renamed it the Western Newspaper Union. It was an auxiliary printing company, meaning that it sold reams of newsprint with preprinted news on one side so that newspaper editors could fill the blank side with local news. Later, the company sold stereotype plates that had feature stories that newspaper editors could buy for use.[73]

George Joslyn's business did well in Omaha. Eventually, he held a monopoly on the auxiliary printing business east of the Sierra Nevada Mountains. As the couple's wealth grew, they also invested in properties around Omaha. Their growing wealth allowed for a more opulent lifestyle as well. By 1883, they could afford to move into the Metropolitan Hotel, one of two hotels George owned. Three years later, they bought their first home. By 1891, they signaled their elevation into Omaha's wealthy elite with the purchase of a fourteen-room home in the fashionable Kountze Place subdivision. They didn't stay there long, however, as they purchased a five-acre dairy farm in 1893. The farm became the site of their dream home, Lynhurst.[74]

Sarah and George Joslyn's home, Lynhurst, better known as Joslyn Castle, Omaha, Nebraska. *Courtesy of Nikolyn McDonald.*

Construction of Lynhurst, which most people in Omaha simply called "the Castle," began in 1897 with the gatehouse, followed in 1901 with a two-story stone carriage house. Construction on the residence, a thirty-five-room mansion in the Scottish baronial style, began in 1902 and was completed eleven months later. The home included a ballroom, gymnasium, bowling alley, billiard room, conservatory, wine cellar and sauna. It even included a music room with an organ that the Joslyns made available for church recitals and professional performances, since no one in the family played the instrument.[75]

The grounds of Lynhurst were as elaborate as the home. They were laid out in an informal yet lavish style with large flowerbeds and a large greenhouse for exotic plants. Unfortunately, a tornado on Easter Day in 1919 destroyed the greenhouse and George never had the heart to replace it. The Joslyns also paid to have more than one hundred mature trees planted on the grounds of their new home. They placed birdhouses and bird feeding stations throughout. The grounds were ideal for entertaining, and the Joslyns often held events for children, such as their annual Fourth of July party, where George would fire his miniature brass cannon.[76]

The Joslyns had two children. Sarah gave birth to a boy, Clifton Howard, in 1873, but he lived for only three and a half months. Having had no other children of their own, they adopted a young girl, Violet Carl, in Omaha. It is unclear how the Joslyns came to know Violet, although it could have been through a variety of organizations that Sarah supported. The Joslyns also had many extended family members who would often visit, including George's brother, sister, cousin and many nephews.[77]

In their free time, the Joslyns grew a prized orchid collection and did jigsaw puzzles, one of which became part of the fireplace screen in their living room. They also raised and showed horses and dogs. Sarah loved animals and flowers, which she expressed through her charity work and past times. Her daughter, Violet, described her as a "private person who insisted on keeping personal actions and beliefs separate from any public activities." Yet at the same time, Sarah also believed that her family's wealth should be shared directly influenced her public activities.[78]

Sarah's civic involvement started in 1887 when she joined with seven other women to create the Board of Charities for the city of Omaha. Her personal interests were child and animal welfare, but her advocacy extended beyond these areas into the reform of prisons and mental health institutions, support for drug addiction treatment facilities and women's suffrage. Sarah was a lifelong supporter of the Child Saving Institute, which looked to provide for orphan, dependent or homeless children. She was also one of the most prominent members of the Humane Society in Omaha, which worked toward the prevention of cruelty to both animals and children. The group elected her as a national officer, and in 1912 she was one of seven members of the Humane Society commissioned as "humane and traffic officers" of the Omaha Volunteer Police Force.[79]

George's philanthropy took the form of large financial donations. Besides the organizations that Sarah was actively involved in, the couple gave generously to the University of Omaha, the Unitarian Church and the Old People's Home. Many of their donations went to new buildings. In 1909, the couple gave $25,000, equivalent to nearly $1 million today, to the Child Saving Institute for a new building. It was the largest charitable donation in Omaha to that date. In 1916, with the University of Omaha outgrowing its current home, the Joslyns pledged $25,000 toward a new building. Their donation was matched, allowing the university to construct a new building, Joslyn Hall, to house the college. After her husband's death, Sarah Joslyn gave money to the university for another new building. She also financed a new headquarters for the Humane Society, which included the first small animal hospital in Nebraska. Sarah's charity also extended to the arts. She helped found the Omaha Community Playhouse in 1924. The players performed their first play in 1925 but didn't have their own theater until Sarah donated land at Fortieth and Davenport Streets for a temporary theater. The site housed the playhouse until 1959.[80]

Sarah Joslyn's work did not stop there. During World War I, she volunteered with the National League of Women's Service, a newly created organization supporting the war effort by arranging for volunteer women to take over the jobs of departing soldiers. Following her love of animals, the group raised money by making horse socks: carpet and burlap "slippers" for horses' hooves that gave them better traction. The group sold the horse socks in drugstores, and they were especially popular with teamsters. Sarah also opened her home to soldiers stationed at Fort Omaha for rest and relaxation, offering that they were welcome to come "smoke, bowl, play billiards, read, lounge, chat, play the Victrola, listen to the pipe organ or do anything else that they want."[81]

Sarah's greatest gift to the city of Omaha, however, was the Joslyn Memorial. Her husband, George, died on October 4, 1916, at home with Sarah and Violet at his bedside. When he died, he was the richest man in

Nebraska with an estate valued at over $6 million, the equivalent of over $110 million today. It was nearly twice the size of the next-largest estate ever probated in Nebraska at that time, that of Sarah Emily Creighton's husband, John. After bequests were made, Sarah was still left with $5.5 million, making her the wealthiest woman in the state. She was determined to spend the money in Omaha. When asked why she didn't take the money and move to somewhere with a better climate, she responded, "The money was made in Omaha and it will be spent here."[82]

While volunteering at the 1893 Trans-Mississippi Exposition in Omaha, Sarah was on the Entertainment Bureau, which highlighted culture and art in Omaha. The experience made her aware of Omaha's need for a museum. She volunteered at art exhibits at the public library and worked on a Fine Arts Society drive in 1914 to raise money to buy the Turner Mansion and convert it to a museum. Unfortunately, the Society couldn't raise enough money and abandoned the project. Another attempt at building an art museum attached to a new library failed in 1920 due to lack of support for replacing the current library.[83] In 1922, Sarah announced her intention to build an art museum as a memorial to her late husband. The new museum would be a center for art, music and other cultural activities. She told the *Morning World-Herald*, "I have wanted to do something for Omaha, because it is my home, my friends are here, and it is the city I love….My only hope is that the

Postcard image of Joslyn Memorial, Omaha, Nebraska. *Eric Nelson News Company.*

building will be of use and benefit to the public, and that it will do the people some good."[84]

Sarah funded the new museum by selling most of her stock in the Western Newspaper Union to the officers of the company. Many even viewed this act as charity because she was giving the business to the employees rather than selling to someone else. She broke ground for the new museum in 1928, and the Joslyn Memorial opened on November 29, 1931. The museum included galleries, a marble fountain court and a concert hall with the organ from the Joslyn home. The memorial was a success. Approximately twenty-five thousand people visited on the first day, and by 1938, it was listed as one of the one hundred best buildings in the United States. Sarah remained involved in the operations of Joslyn Memorial until the end of her life. She chose the Memorial's trustees and served as president of the board. She also organized a library arts society and bought the painting *Portrait of Miss Franks* for the art collection.[85]

Sarah Joslyn received many accolades. In 1928, Omaha Post No. 1 of the American Legion named her "Omaha's first citizen." She received an honorary doctors of laws (LLD) degree from the University of Omaha in 1937, the institution's first honorary degree awarded. The university posthumously selected her as one of ten charter members in their Omaha Hall of Fame. In 1975, the Nebraska International Women's Year Coalition inducted her into its Women's Hall of Fame.[86]

Sarah fell ill in late 1939, and though she seemed to rally in the new year, she became sick once again and died at home of a heart attack on February 28, 1940. She left money to Violet, her grandchildren and other close family members, as well as servants and a few friends. She also left thousands of dollars to her favorite charities. Family and friends were allowed to choose items from her personal possessions, and what was left went to the Library Arts Society for maintenance of Joslyn Memorial, which was renamed the Joslyn Art Museum in 1994. Both the museum and Lynhurst, now known as Joslyn Castle, are open to the public to this day.[87]

Mary Lucretia Creighton, Anna Wilson and Sarah Joslyn each left a legacy in Omaha through their philanthropy. Their contributions to education, healthcare, the arts and social welfare have shaped the city's cultural and civic landscape. Mary Lucretia Creighton's bequest led to the founding of Creighton University, while Anna Wilson's controversial yet significant donations supported various charitable organizations. Sarah Joslyn's dedication to the arts and education resulted in the establishment of the Joslyn Art Museum and many other institutions. Together, these women's philanthropic efforts show the powerful role of women in shaping their communities and creating lasting legacies. Their stories provide inspiration for future generations of philanthropists and highlight the importance of giving back to one's community.

4

JOURNALISTS

ELIA PEATTIE AND HARRIET MACMURPHY

The turn of the twentieth century marked a significant period of change and advancement for women. Greater access to education made it possible for more women to pursue professional careers. While many women became teachers, others ventured into journalism, finding opportunities to work for and even manage newspapers. Elizabeth Cochran, famously known as Nellie Bly, paved the way for a new kind of journalist who used her unique female perspective to advocate for women and women's interests. At the same time, the Woman's Club movement gave women an outlet to apply their traditional caretaker role to their larger community. Journalists like Elia Peattie and Harriet MacMurphy reported on the activities of Woman's Clubs and used the social networks they created to bring about social reforms.

In 1880, only 2 percent of journalists were women. Many of these women entered the field because their husbands' owned newspapers. As the nineteenth century ended, however, the buying power women held resulted in companies starting to target their advertising toward women. To increase their ad sales, newspapers began to look for ways to expand their female readership. This resulted in opportunities for women to write columns on food, fashion and family. By 1900, the percentage of women involved in journalism in the United States had risen to 7 percent.[88]

Despite the growth of women in journalism, newspaperwomen faced significant challenges in a male-dominated field. Women journalists often struggled to gain respect and faced skepticism about their abilities. Stories of women like Lena Spear and Rosa Hudspeth illustrate the difficulties they faced, including being overlooked in their own offices and having to prove their capability to run a newspaper. Lena Spear held typesetter jobs through high school and a week after graduation started publishing the *Central City Democrat*, yet in 1902 she told the Nebraska Press Association:

> *At home I have often had the experience of having a stranger enter the office, take no notice of me at the desk, but look around until he found a boy or a tramp printer reading the exchanges and inquire of this representative of the male persuasion if he were the editor.*[89]

Five years later, Rosa Hudspeth, proprietor of the *Stuart Ledger*, shared the challenge a woman editor faced in finding laborers for her paper:

> *As an employer of printers, if she is hazardous enough to enter the profession without a protector, she will meet things that will terrify any woman without a heart full of Nebraska grit, the martyr spirit of a Fiji missionary and the power of encasing herself in a shell as hard and impenetrable as the shell of a turtle.*[90]

One printer informed Hudspeth "that a woman had neither the nerve nor the physical endurance to run a paper and do the mechanical work," therefore, he insisted on a contract giving him editorial power over the newspaper. Unsurprisingly, his job did not last long.[91]

Women reporters, too, dealt with low pay, limited assignments and infrequent recognition for their work. Some women, such as Mora Balcombe and Viola Pratt, had to get by writing freelance articles. Others could only get jobs writing certain types of columns viewed as appropriate for women to write. For example, Willa Cather (chapter 9) could only get a job writing theater reviews for the *Lincoln Courier*.[92] Annie L. Miller, a reporter with the *Nebraska State Journal* around the turn of the century, commented on how her editor always gave her the "uninteresting minor assignments" typically given "to the greenest reporter." Despite the limited opportunities, journalism gave women a voice in society. Miller herself noted that her society columns about "trivialities" could cause more angst in the community than any national news. She said:

> *A gentleman of intelligence and culture has been known to appear as chagrined as a defeated politician because of the omission of his wife's*

name from the report of an important function, and the leaving out of a name of an assisting lady at a reception has more than once aroused the suspicion that the hostess had taken this method of stabbing a friend in the back.[93]

Some women used their newspapers to influence society and advocate for change. Examples include Nebraska newspaperwomen Mary Fairbrother, editor and printer of the *Women's Weekly*, the official newspaper of the Nebraska Woman's Club, and Clara Bewick Colby (see chapter 2), who published the *Woman's Tribune*, the mouthpiece of the national woman's suffrage movement. Newspaperwoman Maggie Eberhart Mobley was institutionalized during the 1890s for mental problems. After her release, she used her newspaper to share the poor conditions and ill treatment she had received while in the mental institution.[94]

Elia Peattie and Harriet MacMurphy, prominent Nebraska journalists during the late nineteenth and early twentieth centuries, are further examples of how women in journalism used their voices to champion social reform. Both women were also instrumental in developing the Woman's Club movement in Nebraska and used the state organization to encourage reforms. Peattie, known for her editorial work and social commentary, and MacMurphy, known for her contributions to food safety reform, both played crucial roles in advancing women's roles in journalism as well as broader societal change.

Elia Peattie (1862–1935) was one of the more prolific women journalists in Nebraska, even though she lived in Omaha for only a handful of years. She referred to herself as the first woman reporter in Omaha. Her writings are still significant for their social insight and advocacy, reflecting the dynamic changes of the late nineteenth and early twentieth centuries, especially in the lives of women. Peattie was born Elia Wilkinson in Kalamazoo, Michigan, but her family moved to the Chicago area when she was ten. She attended school until the seventh grade, when she had to drop out to help her father set type at his job-printing business. Although her formal education ended at that point, she continued to teach herself by reading the dictionary.[95]

In 1882, at the age of twenty, she went to live with a cousin in Chicago after suffering a case of "nervous prostration" while caring for her invalid mother and four sisters. She never returned to her parents' home, marrying Robert Burns Peattie in 1883. She had met Robert five years earlier at a dance. At the time of their marriage, he was a reporter for the *Chicago Tribune*.

They went on to have four children together: Edward, Barbara, Roderick and Donald.[96]

One reason the couple's marriage worked so well was that Robert supported Elia's desire to write. She published her first poem in the *Chicago Times*, "Ode to Neptune," in 1882. Her writing career began with short stories, including a popular Christmas story published in the *Chicago Tribune* in 1885. After Elia won several short-story contests at the paper, the editor decided it was cheaper just to hire her full time. She started in 1886, the second "girl" reporter in Chicago, and was assigned to the Art and Society page. While she had no experience with art and her writing still needed work, she eagerly took to the job and excelled at it. As reporter for the *Tribune*, she interviewed prominent figures of her day, exposed fraudulent spiritualists, traveled as a correspondent throughout the Midwest and wrote for the Sunday edition—all of this while raising her young family.[97]

The Peatties moved to Omaha in 1888 when Robert accepted a position as managing editor of the *Omaha Daily Herald*. Elia urged him to take the position because they had also offered her a position as a columnist, with a byline—a rarity for women reporters at that time. The next year, the *Daily Herald* merged with the *Omaha Daily World* to become the *Omaha World-Herald*. Elia wrote for the paper until 1896 and became their chief editorial writer during her tenure. Her first column, "A Word with the Women," focused on everything from local life to social commentary. In 1890, she started a column called "What Women Are Doing."[98]

Peattie's column covered a wide range of topics, from a day at the Omaha stockyards to applauding the work of charitable institutions in the city. It was her social commentary, however, that set her apart. She addressed public issues like education, vigilante lynchings and poor conditions for working women. She also supported women's suffrage and the concept of the "New Woman." The New Woman movement started in the 1890s and lasted until around 1920. New women were those who chose careers over the more traditional roles of wife and mother. In 1895, Peattie responded to a *World-Herald* editorial condemning the "New Woman" with her own article "In Defense of Her Own Sex," defending the nobility of women who sought life beyond home and hearth:

> *I have seen women who could not narrow themselves to domesticity. However much they might envy those women who could be happy by a fireside, they themselves could not, but were impelled by some great power to immolate themselves for humanity. Some of these have been in convents, some have*

been in hospitals, some in pulpits, and some in teachers' chairs. They felt a "call" to their wide vocation.... They are isolated and remarkable beings who are thus impelled to the unusual, and since they are disinterested, and even suffer martyrdom for their convictions, one cannot afford to disbelieve in the "call" though one may be commonplace one's self, and never have responded to any sort of a call unless it be the dinner bell.[99]

Peattie also used her columns to report on the activity of Woman's Clubs, especially the Omaha Woman's Club, which she helped establish. The Woman's Club movement started in 1868 when newspaper columnist Jane Croly founded the woman's club Sorosis in New York. The movement didn't catch on until the 1880s, however, and exploded in the 1890s. These clubs often began as literary societies focused on the arts but grew into community service organizations focused on various social and civic concerns. They offered middle- and upper-class women a supportive community, a place to further their self-education, and an outlet to serve their communities in ways that aligned with their primary duties as homemakers.[100]

In 1893, Peattie wrote an article suggesting the creation of a Woman's Club in Omaha. The column met with an overwhelming response that resulted in the Omaha Woman's Club. Within a year, the club's membership was well over four hundred. Peattie represented the Omaha club at the General Federation of Woman's Clubs in Philadelphia in 1894 and helped form the Nebraska State Federation of Women's Clubs. Nebraska was the seventh state to join the national organization. Peattie's column promoted the Omaha club and served as a newsletter for the group. She also traveled across the state to help form local clubs and wrote about them in her column.[101]

Elia Peattie was also well known for her literary work. She was a frequent contributor to literary magazines such as *Lippincott's, Cosmopolitan, St. Nicholas* and *Harper's Weekly*. In 1888, a Chicago publishing company commissioned her to write a children's book, *The Story of America: Containing the Romantic Incidents of History, from the Discovery of American to the Present Time*. She produced the seven-hundred-page work in four months, dictating to two stenographers. The following year, the Northwestern Railroad Company hired her to write a travel book for their Minneapolis to Seattle and Tacoma route, as well as their steamship line to Alaska. Railroad companies used these types of guides as advertisements. Peattie's *A Journey Through Wonderland: Or, the Pacific Northwest and Alaska, with a Description of the Country Traversed by the Northern Pacific Railroad* came out in 1890. She took a more creative approach to the typical travel narrative by creating a fictional subplot about Scott Key, a young New York businessman, who was traveling the route for the first time. Also in 1890, she completed a murder mystery set in Chicago called *The Judge*. It won a $900 prize from the *Detroit Free Press* and was published by Rand McNally. The money allowed the Peatties to move into a home of their own.[102]

A Populist, Peattie campaigned for Williams Jennings Bryan and in 1892 helped another journalist, Thomas Henry Tibbles, husband of Susette LaFlesche Tibbles (chapter 6), write a pamphlet supporting Free Silver. Influenced by Tibbles's description of the difficult plight of farmers on Nebraska's prairie, Peattie authored the story "Jim Lancy's Waterloo" about the failed attempt of a farmer to make his living on the Nebraska prairie. *Cosmopolitan* magazine later printed the story, and it appeared in Peattie's short story collection, *A Mountain Woman*. The Populist Party also used the story as propaganda.[103]

During the winter of 1890, Robert became critically ill with double pneumonia. His health never recovered, and frequent absences for recovery cost him his job at the *Omaha World-Herald*. He briefly found work at a Council Bluffs, Iowa newspaper before leaving for New York City to try his luck there. He eventually ended up back in Chicago. Peattie found her relationship with the men at the *World-Herald* strained after her husband's departure, so in 1896, she decided to join her husband in Chicago.[104] She penned her farewell column of "A Word with the Women" on October 11, 1896, praising the growth in women's journalism in Omaha:

> *I have just written that familiar headline for the last time....When I first came to Omaha newspaper women were not common here. People suspected that women would not make practical newspaper workers.... But since that time women have become well known on the newspapers in Omaha, and there are several efficient women writers engaged on various papers of the city.*[105]

Although Elia Peattie never again lived in Nebraska, she visited over the years to lecture. She died in 1935 while visiting her grandchildren in Vermont. In 2007, the Nebraska Press Associated voted her into their Hall of Fame.[106]

HARRIET DAKIN MACMURPHY (1848–1932) was a contemporary of Peattie, a well-known Nebraska newspaperwoman, and was also involved in the Omaha Woman's Club. With over fifty years in the Nebraska newspaper business, she earned the title "dean of Nebraska newspaper women."[107] It was said of her: "She knows a newspaper in all its departments from the composing room to the editorial sanctum and has done everything about it from inking the roller to writing editorials."[108]

Harriet was born in Waukesha, Wisconsin, in 1848, as one of twelve children. When she was eleven, her family moved to Nebraska, with Harriet bringing up the rear of their caravan driving a buggy and leading the family's prize stock. The family settled in Decatur, on the edge of the Omaha Indian Reservation. It was there that she became friends with the wife of Henry Fontenelle, brother of Logan Fontenelle, the grandson of one of the last Omaha chiefs, Big Elk. MacMurphy later documented this friendship and what she learned from the Omaha people in her book *The Story of the Fontenelles*. For a time, Harriet served as governess for the children of the Omaha reservation's Indian's agent, Robert Furnas, and then entered Brownell Hall, Omaha's first boarding school for women. It was while at Brownell that she wrote her first newspaper article, which was published in the *Omaha Daily Herald*. According to newspaper accounts, she would have been the first girl to graduate from the school had she not had to drop out because of financial issues.[109]

Harriet's newspaper career started with her marriage to John A. MacMurphy in 1867. Not long after their marriage, he became a reporter for the *Omaha Republican*. Sometime after that he bought the first of what would become many newspapers that he ran over the years, with Harriet working at his side. The couple ran newspapers in cities around southeastern Nebraska, including Blair, Plattsmouth, Schuyler, Wahoo, South Omaha, Geneva and Beatrice. Harriet regularly played a role in the newspaper business, becoming the "devil of the office" and "doing everything from setting type to addressing the weekly mailing list by hand."[110] When they owned the South Omaha newspaper *Hoof and Horn*, she kept the books and read proof. While in Beatrice, she wrote the social column for their paper. During the early 1890s, she began writing for the *Omaha World-Herald* on domestic science. She continued working for the *World-Herald* after her husband's death in 1898, eventually becoming their domestic science editor. Her editorials appeared in newspapers around the state and in the East. She finally retired from newspaper work in 1925.[111]

Like Peattie, MacMurphy also advocated for the formation of a woman's club in Omaha and was a founding member. She was the first head of the Omaha club's domestic science department. Later, she became secretary of the household economics department of the General Federation of Woman's Clubs. Harriet's leadership in the early days of the state woman's club had a national influence. During her tenure, she led a national effort to pass pure food and drug laws in the United States.

MacMurphy first heard about the issue of food purity when she traveled around the country with her "model kitchen." This model kitchen originated as an exhibit for the 1893 Trans-Mississippi Exhibition in Omaha. She used it to show the many ways to use corn products for food. She famously had one hundred ways to prepare corn, and her cornbread recipe was especially popular. While demonstrating her one hundred ways to cook corn at the Buffalo Exposition, MacMurphy met food scientists and learned about the hazards of adulterated food. This was all the impetus she needed to take up the cause. She started to speak to others about pure food and the need for a pure food law. When the pure food law was at risk of failing before Congress, she encouraged the members of General Federation of Women's Clubs to contact their congressmen to keep the bill alive.[112]

What Mrs. Harriet MacMurphy, State Food Inspector, says:

"Kuenne's Bakery, at 2916 Leavenworth, is well kept and also has a shower bath in the basement for the employees."

We Invite You to Inspect Our Bake Shop.

KUENNE'S BAKERY
2916 Leavenworth St.

Advertisement for the Kuenne Bakery, supported by Harriet S. McMurphy, state food inspector. *From The Omaha (NE) Daily News, September 10, 1908.*

HARRIET S. MACMURPHY, the State Food and Drug Inspector, in a recent statement, asserts that **SKINNER'S MACARONI** is a **"Perfect Food,"** that it contains large percentages of all the nutritive elements which constitute **Food Value.**
At the bottom of this page you will find a coupon which is worth **FIVE CENTS** to **You.** Cut it out—present it to your grocer with a nickel—and get a full 10-cent size of **SKINNER'S MACARONI** (**Mezzani**) **or SPAGHETTI.** Then write to us and we will send you a new book containing one hundred of Mrs. MacMurphy's BEST RECIPES. Send a postal for this book **today**—**They are going fast.**

Advertisement for Skinner Macaroni, supported by Harriet S. MacMurphy, the state food and drug inspector. *From The Omaha (NE) Daily News, August 14, 1911.*

Passage of the Pure Food and Drug Act of 1906 wasn't enough for MacMurphy, however. She was also determined to be a food inspector. She told the State Woman's Club Federation: "This is a woman's bill. We helped to have it passed. I believe we inspired it. It affects us more directly than it does the men. I want to be food and drug inspector for the state."[113] With the club's support, she succeeded when Nebraska Governor George L. Sheldon appointed her, and she became the first woman food inspector in the United States. She inspected food production and sale throughout the state, except for milk, including packinghouses, creameries, cold storage plants, local shops, groceries, meat markets and bakeries. Later, when the state combined food and drug inspection, she also inspected liquor, which was considered a drug. "I think I have visited every saloon in Nebraska in my day," she told the *Omaha Morning World-Herald* in 1926, "and I was never insulted in one." MacMurphy held the state food inspector position under three governors, until the fourth, John H. Morehead, decided not to have a woman in the position. He appointed a man over the protest of many women in the state.[114]

Harriet MacMurphy held other firsts in Nebraska besides being the first state food inspector. She was also the first president of the Omaha Women's Press Club and the first permanent secretary of the Nebraska Press Association. Besides these accomplishments, she was also a member of the Woman's Christian Temperance Union and the Young Women's Christian Association and was active in the Political Equity League, Nebraska Writers Guild, the Academy of Sciences and the Nebraska Pioneers Association. Elia Peattie said of MacMurphy, "She can be relied upon for the most accurate information concerning pioneer times that is to be found outside the pages of the reports of the Nebraska Historical Society."[115]

During her last year as food inspector, she took a 480-acre homestead in the Sandhills and named it Dakin's Ranch. Later, she built a cottage, Ti

Zhinga, on Fog Crook Boulevard with the oldest oak in Fontenelle forest in her yard. Not far from her cottage was the grave of Logan Fontenelle. MacMurphy died at the age of eighty-three in Los Angeles, where she was living with her sister after having moved there six years prior.[116]

Elia Peattie and Harriet MacMurphy, along with the many other female journalists in Nebraska, show how journalism provided a crucial platform for women to influence society and champion reforms. These women not only excelled in their professional careers but also used their social networks, formed through organizations such as woman's clubs to advocate for social reforms to drive change. Peattie, with her incisive social commentary, and MacMurphy, with her leadership in pure food and drug laws, exemplified how women used the means they had at hand to change society in a positive way. These trailblazing women, through their dedication and advocacy, paved the way for future generations, proving that women could be formidable forces for good within their communities and beyond. Their legacy underscores the profound influence of women's contributions to journalism and social reform during this transformative period.

5

CIVIL RIGHTS ACTIVISTS

OPHELIA CLENLANS, JESSIE HALE-MOSS AND MILDRED BROWN

A frican American women were pivotal in the civil rights movement in
Nebraska, especially in Omaha. They played critical roles in uniting
and supporting their community as it faced racial discrimination.
From early activists like Ophelia Clenlans and Jessie Hale-Moss to mid-
twentieth-century community leader Mildred Brown, these women called
attention to inequalities and advocated for justice and equal opportunity.
These trailblazing women were leaders in their community and played a
significant role in the history of North Omaha.

Nebraska's African American population has always been relatively
low. Even today, Black people make up less than 5 percent of the state's
population. However, African Americans have been present in Nebraska
since the first territorial census in 1854, which listed four African American
slaves. The next year, Sally Bayne, a free Black woman, arrived in Omaha.
She is considered the first free Black person to settle in what would become
the state of Nebraska.[117]

Although slavery was allowed in the early days of the territory,
Nebraska was considered a safe place for Black people after the Civil
War. Many moved here in search of cheap land. Robert Anderson, a
former slave, was the first African American to homestead in Nebraska
in 1870. Other Black settlers arrived during the 1870s as part of the
movement of former slaves homesteading in Kansas and Nebraska,
known as the "Exoduster" migration. This migration resulted in three
predominantly African Americans communities in Nebraska: Overton in

Dawson County in 1885 and Brownlee and DeWitty in Cherry County in the early 1900s. The Black population grew exponentially in Nebraska between 1870 and 1890, from 789 to 8,900.[118]

Many African Americans gravitated toward urban areas in the state, particularly Omaha. They were lured by opportunities to work on the railroads and stockyards, but they usually only found employment as strikebreakers, used to get immigrant workers to agree to lower wages and poor working conditions. In 1892, Elia Peattie (chapter 4) of the *Omaha World-Herald* profiled Omaha's African American community. She noted that the African American community in Omaha had a population of around six thousand, which might not seem much, yet "the percentage of Afro-Americans on the streets of this city appears to be large." She attributed this to the community being "persons of independence, activity and a greater or less degree of importance." Peattie wanted Omahans to see the African American community not as "other" but as part of the larger Omaha community. Their children attended public schools and the women were mostly homemakers, with few employed outside the home. The men were employed in various pursuits, but she argued that their employment was not as varied as it could be if they were only afforded certain opportunities otherwise denied to them because of their race. For example, there were no African American merchants in Omaha. There were, however, three Black men on the police force, a Black mail clerk at the post office and four Black mail carriers. One of the mail carriers, E.R. Overall, was also president of the Missouri and Nebraska Coal Mining Company, active in politics and the labor movement.[119]

Overall, Peattie painted picture of a solid African American community, with its own leadership, newspaper, churches and community organizations. Despite the positive portrait Peattie portrayed, it hid the prejudice and threat of violence that Black people faced in Omaha in the late nineteenth century. Only the year before, Peattie had used her column to denounce vigilante justice in Omaha. Her article was partially in response to the beating and lynching of Joe Coe, a Black man accused of raping a white woman.[120]

The early Omaha African American community included many prominent women. OPHELIA "CELIA" CLENLANS (1841–1907) was a contemporary of Peattie and an early advocate for racial equality in Omaha. Clenlans was born a slave in Platte County, Missouri, and later moved to Omaha, where she married Emanuel S. Clenlans and had a daughter, Laura. She was an active member of the African American community in North Omaha around the turn of the twentieth century. In 1896, she held a position on the executive board of the National Federal of Afro-American Women. She was also a member of the Omaha Colored Women's Club, a club created when the newly organized Omaha Woman's Club (see chapter 4) denied Black women membership.[121] She is notable for an article she wrote in the *Omaha World-Herald* in 1901 about the segregation of clubs for women. While acknowledging gratitude for the assistance of her "white sisters," she argued that Black women only wanted "to learn of them that we may better enable to help ourselves and our families." Clenlans continued, "Shame on a woman who is afraid to take another woman by the and say, 'God bless you in your noble work.'"[122] Although other Woman's Clubs, such as the one in Chicago, had allowed in Black women, Omaha's Woman's Club was far more reluctant. While some members, like Elia Peattie, were in favor of including all women, many feared the new organization might not survive the controversial move of admitting African American members.[123]

OMAHA'S AFRICAN AMERICAN POPULATION grew substantially in the early twentieth century. Several factors led to the mass migration of Black people from the South to more northern states, called the Great Migration. Immigration restrictions starting in 1917 gave more employment opportunities to African Americans in northern factories, stockyards and railroads. Meanwhile, hostile conditions in the South between Jim Crow laws, police brutality and lynchings also contributed to the migration. The Black population in Omaha doubled between 1910 and 1920, from just over five thousand to over ten thousand people.[124]

Although conditions in Omaha might have been better for African Americans than they would have experienced in the South, they still faced prejudice and exclusion. Omaha increasingly became segregated over the decades between 1890 and 1930. At the turn of the century, the Black community coexisted in downtown Omaha's central business district beside other ethnic enclaves, such as the Irish, Scandinavians, Germans, Italians and Eastern European Jews. After 1920, the Black population began moving to North Omaha due to fear of racial violence and central Omaha becoming a vice district. Later zoning laws and housing covenants ensured segregation by preventing African Americans from moving into white neighborhoods. Black residents were effectively restricted to the Near North Side neighborhood.[125]

Despite there being more jobs available, Black residents of Omaha had limited options for employment. Generally, they found work in dangerous or dirty industries that others didn't want. These jobs were menial, entry level and low paying, with little or no opportunity for advancement. One-third of the men in Omaha's Near North Side worked in the meatpacking plants and another fourth worked on the railroad yards. Others worked as domestics, waiters, janitors and porters. Black women also often had to work or take in boarders to make ends meet. In the first half of the twentieth century, Black women in Omaha held jobs as servants in white households, hotel housekeepers and elevator operators.[126]

Racial violence also became an issue during this period. In September 1919, a crowd of angry white people brutally beat, lynched and then burned William Brown, a Black man accused of raping a white woman. This act of violence had a profound effect on the Black community, resulting in its relocation to North Omaha. It also brought about the birth of the African American civil rights movement in Omaha. JESSIE HALE-MOSS (1880–1920) was one of the leaders of this movement. She was a businesswoman, newspaper editor and one of the first leaders of the Omaha National Association for the Advancement of Colored People (NAACP).[127]

Hale-Moss was born in Middleport, Ohio, and graduated from Middleport High School in 1893. She taught public school for several years before moving to Nebraska with her husband around 1911. In Omaha, she sold real estate and managed the Kashmir Beauty Shop. Hale-Moss's involvement in Omaha's nascent civil rights movement began before the lynching of Will Brown. She was actively involved in the fledgling Omaha NAACP, first as secretary, and then in 1918 as president. Through the NAACP she advocated for Omaha newspapers to stop white supremacist coverage of the African American community when they began printing anti–African American propaganda following race riots in other large cities. She led a letter-writing campaign calling attention to the anti-Black male coverage in the media and unwarranted and unjust arrests of Black men by the Omaha police. She also led the Omaha NAACP's support of more than thirty Black men who had been accused of attacking white women. All the men were found innocent except one, Will Brown. She called on the Omaha City Council to let her present evidence of how the media was harming Black men, but her requests were ignored. After the lynching, she and Reverend John Albert Williams telephoned around the African American community in Omaha to warn them to stay indoors to avoid further violence.[128]

Advertisement for the Omaha Branch of the National Association for the Advancement of Colored People (NAACP) noting Mrs. Jessie Hale Moss as secretary. *From The Monitor (Omaha, NE), May 10, 1919.*

After the lynching of Will Brown, Hale-Moss was a driving force in creating the Negro Christian Women's Association, also known as the North Side YWCA, and became an assistant editor in a short-lived Black newspaper called the *New Era*. She also campaigned for African American women's suffrage in 1920. Unfortunately, her work was cut short when she died suddenly at the age of forty on November 14, 1920.[129] *The Monitor*, an Omaha newspaper, commented on her death that:

Jessie Hale-Moss is a woman whom Omaha will sadly miss. She was a zealous, self-sacrificing and unremitting worker for any cause which enlisted her interest and sympathy and every movement which affected her race had her whole-hearted devotion.[130]

Among her many accomplishments, Jessie Hale-Moss is also remembered as a founder of the North Omaha's Colored Old Folks' Home; director of the Cooperative Workers of America, a Black-owned department store; secretary of the Douglas County Colored Women's Republican Club; and a member of Dubois Players, an African American theater group that performed at small parties in North Omaha. She was also an advocate for poor and needy boys and girls in the North Omaha community. Her positive effect on the community continued long after her death.[131]

ALTHOUGH JESSIE HALE-MOSS'S EFFORTS were cut short, others took up the charge of advancing civil rights in Omaha in the following decades. One of the most prominent civil rights activists in Omaha after World War II was newspaperwoman MILDRED BROWN (1905–1989). Brown not only was a voice for equal opportunity for Black people in Omaha but also supported the community through her newspaper, the *Omaha Star*, and was the matriarch of the Near North Side African American community in Omaha.[132]

Brown was born in Bessemer, Alabama. Her father was a pastor, and her mother supplemented the family's income making door-to-door sales. Mildred later claimed to have learned her love for sales from her mother, who often took her daughter with her when making rounds. Brown's great-grandparents were an interracial couple in post–Civil War Alabama. Unable to marry because he was a white plantation owner and she was a freed slave, they cohabitated, which became an issue only when their sons had to fight in court to inherit their father's property. Because of this ancestry and inheritance, her family was part of the Black upper middle class in Bessemer.

The Brown family moved to Birmingham, Alabama, when Mildred was young. She graduated from Miles Memorial High School and College in 1924 with a pre-normal teaching certificate for elementary and secondary instruction and returned to Bessemer to teach elementary school. In 1927, she married Shirley Edward Gilbert, a pharmacy student, in Pulaski, Tennessee. Mildred wanted to keep teaching while he finished school, so they kept their marriage a secret. After he graduated, like many African Americans at the time, they moved north in search of better opportunities.[133]

They first settled in Chicago, where Shirley Edward started his pharmacy career and Mildred pursued higher education. She attended Crane Junior College and the Chicago Normal School with plans to return to Bessemer to resume teaching. That changed when her husband was offered a job at a pharmacy in an upscale drugstore in a Black community in Des Moines, Iowa. The couple moved again in 1933 when Shirley Edward became chief pharmacist of his own pharmacy in the only African American–owned drugstore in Sioux City, Iowa. Mildred worked at the lunch counter at the drugstore and was active in her church. The couple also founded the Booker T. Washington Club to help new arrivals in their Black neighborhood.[134]

While in Sioux City, their church's traveling pastor brought two changes to the couple's life. First, they informally adopted Pastor Harris's thirteen-year-old daughter, Ruth. Ruth's mother had died, and her father wanted a more stable life for her than his job could provide. Second, Pastor Harris told Mildred that the Lord wanted her to start a newspaper. He had noticed her talent for sales, which was necessary to get advertisers to keep a newspaper running. Mildred reached out to other local Black businesses and in 1935 published the first edition of a weekly newspaper, the *Silent Messenger*. It was Brown's first step into the world of newspaper publishing. The next step came a year later when Charles Chapman "C.C" Galloway visited with Mildred and her husband over the holidays. Galloway was the founder and publisher of the *Omaha Guide*, a newspaper that served the Black community in Omaha. The Gilbert's were eager for a new opportunity, as their financial situation had taken a turn for the worst. When Galloway offered them a job, they moved to Omaha.[135]

When they arrived in Omaha, it had a Black population of 13,166 and was the largest Black community they had lived in since leaving Alabama. Shirley Edward started writing for the *Omaha Guide*, and Mildred served as advertising manager. After eighteen months with the *Omaha Guide*, the Gilberts parted ways with Galloway because of creative differences. They had an idea to start their own weekly newspaper, the *Omaha Star*. They bought an office building, which they moved into, and hired many people they had worked with on the *Guide*. The first edition of their weekly paper appeared on July 9, 1938. Unlike the *Guide*, which covered national news

Omaha Star Building at 2216 North Twenty-Fourth Street, Omaha, Nebraska. *Courtesy of Nikolyn McDonald.*

with a more political focus, the Gilberts wanted their newspaper to focus on the local Black community.[136]

Ultimately, the *Omaha Star* became even more successful than the *Omaha Guide* because of its attention to the local community. The paper emphasized positive local news, including engagements and weddings, birth announcements, club meetings and church events. It was one of the few Black newspapers to do so. Mildred knew her customers and what they wanted to read about.[137] She later reflected:

> *People do not buy a newspaper just because it is being printed. They buy a paper if it publishes pictures and names of their brothers and sisters and aunts and uncles. Then they can't get enough copies to send out to their relatives.*[138]

While the newspaper succeeded, Mildred's marriage did not. Mildred filed for divorce upon learning that her husband was having an affair. The divorce was final in 1943. Mildred restored her name to Brown and retained ownership of the *Omaha Star.* Brown devoted herself to her business, viewing it as a ministry to the community. She paid off the loan on the newspaper office and expanded the paper to include society and children's pages. Always looking to increase circulation, she promoted the paper and public events in the community.[139] Brown saw persistence of the Black press as a necessity:

> *If the Negro is deprived of his press, all of the torturous gains achieved through the years since his emancipation will be lost, and tomorrow's Negro youth will be at the mercy of the powerful forces, North and South, that still man the ramparts of bigotry, prejudice and discrimination.*[140]

She recognized the power she held and felt a responsibility to use it for the good of the community, which she did through speaking up for civil rights.

Mildred used her newspaper as a voice against race discrimination for fifty years. She once commented, "I've been up against some stiff obstacles and I have no fear. This paper broke down discrimination in this town. They called us troublemakers, nothing but troublemakers. I just sold ads like mad."[141] One of the first battles she waged was for equal employment opportunities. During the 1930s and '40s, national Black newspapers fought discrimination through consumer campaigns such as the "Don't Buy Where You Can't Work" boycotts and "Spend Your Money Where You Can Work" campaigns. The *Omaha Star* reminded its readers, "It is your hard-earned dollar. Make it count by spending it with merchants and firms who show willingness, not by words but by action, to give employment to all Americans, regardless of race." The *Star* further contributed to these campaigns by encouraging the Black community to shop at a list of the only white-owned businesses in North Omaha that had Black employees.[142]

During the late 1940s, Brown partnered with the DePorres Club, a civil rights group started on the Creighton University campus. Jesuit John Markoe started the club in 1947 to combat local racial discrimination in Omaha after seeing the same discrimination in St. Louis. He wanted to use the club to teach young Black and white women and men to be civil rights activists. While most DePorres Club members were white, the membership also included many African Americans that became influential members of the community, such as Bertha Calloway, a longtime activist, historian and founder of the Negro History Society and Great Plains Black History Museum. Another member, Elizabeth

Pittman, was the first African American female graduate of Creighton Law School. She later became the first African American on the Omaha School Board and was the first woman and first African American judge in the state of Nebraska.[143]

Brown's involvement with the DePorres Club started when her adopted son-in-law, Marvin Kellogg Sr., filed a discrimination suit against the downtown Greyhound Bus Station's Cafe. The café had refused service to Kellogg's interracial party of six, of which Brown was one. The DePorres Club hosted a rally to help pay for Kellogg's legal fees, and Mildred's newspaper publicized the event. From then on, Brown became a staunch ally and mother figure for the group. When the club had to find a location off campus to meet, she provided space in her newspaper office. She also printed summaries of their weekly minutes, featured articles on their activities, published editorials written by club members and hired the club's first president, Denny Holland, at her newspaper.[144]

With the DePorres Club, Brown continued the fight for equal employment opportunities for African Americans in Omaha. The *Omaha Star* regularly printed invitations to discuss the lack of employment opportunities in Omaha at the local YWCA in 1947 and 1948. Brown used the *Star* to report on local businesses that refused to hire Black people. For example, she highlighted the Near North Side Edholm-Sherman Laundry, which refused to hire Black employees even though 70 percent of their clientele were African American. The proprietor told a DePorres Club member it was their policy because white customers might object to being served by a Black person. Brown warned them that they had the right to hire whomever they wanted, but if they didn't change, the *Star* would advocate for a boycott of the business. Her warning resulted in the owners putting the business up for sale.[145]

In 1952, the DePorres Club affiliated with the Congress of Racial Equality (CORE) and elected Brown as their CORE spokesperson. Her first task was to present the club's arguments to the Omaha City Council to encourage the Omaha and Council Bluffs Street Railway Company to hire Black bus drivers. The council brushed aside her arguments with the typical concern that "no white woman would be safe on a street car if there was a black [man] driving." The club responded by printing and distributing pamphlets that provided the home addresses and phone numbers of company officials to irate readers. They also arranged a bus boycott, nearly four years before the famous Montgomery, Alabama bus boycott of 1955–56. It wasn't until the city gave in and threatened to attach an anti-discrimination amendment to the railway's franchise agreement that the company hired three Black drivers. The *Star* proudly printed a large photo of the new employees to share their success.[146]

One of the last equal employment protests that the *Star* worked with the DePorres Club on was against Reed's Ice Cream Company. Two years after telling a DePorres Club member that they would consider hiring Black employees, they still hadn't, so the club ran a message in the newspaper. Brown participated in a picket of the ice cream shop. Her common-law husband, Max Brownell, collected names of "noncompliant residents" and printed the names of this list of "Uncle Toms supporting white supremacy." The *Star* also promised to print photographs of anyone seen breaking the picket line. Their efforts resulted in very few Black people visiting the store and even hundreds of whites turning away when they learned of the store's "un-American employment policy." After nine months, the store finally gave in and hired Virginia Dixon, although she only worked the 5:00 p.m. to midnight shift.[147]

Brown and the DePorres Club also took on segregation in Omaha public schools. They protested that Black students at Omaha's Central High School were not allowed in some activities at the school, specifically their opera. Brown paid for the printing of four thousand handbills explaining why the organization was protesting the performance. Police stopped the leaflet protest, citing that they were not allowed to distribute flyers on school property, but only after three thousand leaflets had already been handed out. Brown also used her newspaper to confront the school system over not hiring more African American teachers even though there was a shortage of two hundred teachers in the system. Brown continued to use her newspaper to point out the inequities in the school system's hiring practices for years. Omaha didn't fully desegregated its public schools until 1976.[148]

The DePorres Club disbanded in October 1954 after seven years of successful protests. The Citizens Coordinating Committee for Civil Liberties, known as 4CL, replaced the club in 1960. Mildred Brown worked with this group as well, although not as part of its leadership. Her days of picketing businesses were over but not her work for civil rights. During the 1950s, she used her newspaper to fight for equal and fair housing in Omaha by educating her readers about laws around restrictive covenants. Omaha neighborhoods used restrictive covenants to keep African Americans from buying houses in certain neighborhoods. Brown let her readers know that the Supreme Court had ruled such covenants invalid in 1948. Ever the teacher, she explained the nuances of the national ruling and why the restrictions were unenforceable. Although her articles had minimal impact on the segregated housing situation, she was involved in the successful effort to desegregate Peony Park's pool and waterslide in 1968.[149]

During the 1960s, Brown's involvement in the organized civil rights movement waned as the Black Power Movement took precedence. The *Star* remained a voice for change in the community, continuing to share about protest meetings, marches and demands to city officials. Brown continued to use her newspaper to encourage and unify the Black community through this challenging time. During the race riots in the late 1960s, Brown—like Hale-Moss before her—challenged the portrayal of African Americans in the *Omaha World-Herald*. She did not publicize the first Omaha race riot, deliberately wanting to focus on the positives rather than the struggles of the Black community. Faced with a housing crisis and division of the African American community because of a new freeway project, Brown encouraged her readers to look for nonviolent solutions to the problems of Black inequality. Her status in the community was clear when rioters destroyed and vandalized many businesses in North Omaha in 1966 but spared her newspaper's offices.[150]

During her life, Mildred Brown was recognized for her accomplishments both as a businesswoman and activist. Besides being one of only three women inducted into the Omaha Business Hall of Fame during her lifetime, she had the honor of being appointed a goodwill ambassador to East Germany by President Lyndon Johnson during the 1960s. After meeting Brown at a national newspaper publishers meeting, Johnson hailed her as "the only black woman who was the owner-founder of a black newspaper still in existence." As goodwill ambassador, she was tasked with studying human rights violations connected with the Berlin Wall. The NAACP presented her with their "Unsung Heroine" service award in 1981.[151]

Brown died on November 2, 1989. Her death came as a surprise. She had always led people to believe she was younger than her actual years, and with her robust health and constant energy no one considered her elderly. Nevertheless, she died in bed from a combination of illness and coronary atherosclerosis. In 1984, when asked what she wanted to be remembered for, she replied, "As a person who dedicated her life to the youth. As someone who tried to practice what she preached—that all people are alike, regardless of race, creed or color, and as one who has tried to educate people to that."[152]

Page from President Lyndon B. Johnson's daily diary, January 27, 1966, noting Mildred Brown of the *Omaha Star* as one of a group of journalists that met with the president to discuss civil rights. *LBJ Presidential Library*.

Mildren Brown received many posthumous honors. She is recognized as holding the record for the longest-running Black newspaper founded by a Black woman in the United States. Her newspaper is still the only Black newspaper in the state of Nebraska. In 2007, she was inducted into the Nebraska Journalism Hall of Fame and the next year into the new Omaha Press Club Journalism of Excellence Hall of Fame. In 2012, she was inducted into the Nebraska Press Women Hall of Fame. The City of Omaha honored her with the Mildred Brown Strolling Park near her *Omaha Star* office. There is also a Mildred Brown Street in Omaha, and Creighton University has the Mildred Brown Scholarship, which helps journalism students of color. The Mildred D. Brown Study Center, across the street from her newspaper offices, commemorates her commitment to the community.[153]

The history of African American journalists in Nebraska is a testament to their enduring impact on civil rights and community cohesion. These journalists, from early pioneers like Ophelia Clenlans and Jessie Hale-Moss to later figures such as Mildred Brown, used their platforms to fight racial discrimination and advocate for equality. Despite Nebraska's small Black population, these leaders galvanized their communities, fostering a sense of unity and resilience. Their contributions were vital in the face of persistent prejudice and violence, as they provided a voice for the marginalized and worked tirelessly for civil rights advancements. Through their efforts, these women laid a robust foundation for future generations, ensuring that the African American community's struggles and triumphs were documented and remembered.

Statue of Mildred Brown next to the Omaha Star Building, Omaha, Nebraska. *Courtesy of Nikolyn McDonald.*

6

ADVOCATES FOR NATIVE AMERICANS

THE LAFLESCHE SISTERS

The LaFlesche sisters—Susette, Rosalie, Marguerite and Susan—embody the themes of activism, leadership and cultural preservation explored in this book. As members of the Omaha tribe in Nebraska, they were prominent figures who navigated the complex intersection of Native American traditions and the encroaching influences of white settlers. Born into a time of momentous change, the sisters took on roles as educators, journalists, reformers, leaders and advocates for their people.

The LaFlesche sisters were members of a prominent family in the Umo^{n}ho^n, or Omaha, tribe. The Omaha people were one of the many Native American tribes that lived in Nebraska at the time of white settlement, along with the Ponca, Otoe and Missouri, Pawnee, Lakota and Dakota, Arapahoe and Cheyenne. The Umo^{n}ho^n Sacred Legend said that they had come long ago from a region of dense woods and great bodies of water far to the east. Like many northern Plains tribes, they were recent migrants to the region, having moved from the Ohio River Valley to the upper Missouri and the Great Plains by the middle of the eighteenth century. The Umo^{n}ho^n established villages along the Missouri River and traveled out onto the plains to hunt buffalo in the summer. The LaFlesche sisters' father, Joseph LaFlesche Jr., was the last recognized chief of the Omaha tribe. He was one of the leaders who signed the Treaty of 1854 in which the Omaha gave up their hunting grounds and agreed to live on a reservation.[154]

Joseph LaFlesche Jr. was the son of a French trapper and an Omaha or Ponca woman. As a child, he experienced life in white cities like St. Louis as well as among various Native American tribes. He came to believe that the only way that Native Americans would survive was to adapt to white lifestyles. He also spent time with Omaha elders to learn their traditions and ceremonies so that he could understand how to keep their unique culture through this assimilation process. One of the principal Omaha chiefs, Big Elk, shared LaFlesche's concerns for the Omaha. Big Elk had traveled to the East in 1837 as a guest of the U.S. government. After his visit, he warned his people: "There is a coming flood which will soon reach us, and I advise you to prepare for it." With his own son sick and unable to lead the Omaha, Big Elk adopted LaFlesche, who took the Omaha name E-sta-mah-za, or "Iron Eye."[155]

When Big Elk died in 1853, LaFlesche took his place as chief. While Iron Eye worked to find a balance between assimilation with the whites and keeping Omaha culture, not everyone agreed with him, which led to a split in the tribe between the older conservatives and Iron Eye and the "Young Men's Party." Nevertheless, Joseph led by example, converting to Christianity, building a two-story wood-frame house, laying out roads and fencing parcels of land to farm. While he taught his children Omaha traditions and they spoke French and Omaha with their parents, he also prepared them for life outside the tribe. Only his oldest daughter, Susette, was given an Omaha name, In-shta-the-amba, "Bright Eyes." He refused to tattoo or pierce his children in the traditional ways and they were to speak only English among themselves. But most importantly, he saw to his children's education, because he believed education was the key to the tribe's survival.[156]

As was traditional among the Omaha, Joseph took two wives. By Mary Gale, the daughter of an Omaha-Otoe-Iowa woman and army surgeon John Gale, he had four daughters: Susette, Rosalie, Marguerite and Susan. By Ta-in-ne, an Omaha woman, he had one daughter and two sons. All his children were educated at the mission and agency schools, and most attended either the Elizabeth Institute for Young Ladies in New Jersey or the Hampton Normal and Agricultural Institute in Virginia or both. His children were born and grew up in a time of considerable change for many Native American peoples. Susette, the second child and first daughter, was born the year her father signed the treaty that gave up the tribe's hunting grounds and moved them to a reservation. She could remember when her people still went on buffalo hunts in the summer. Yet all of Joseph LaFleche's children by Mary Gale walked a challenging path between embracing a white American lifestyle while still holding on to their Omaha traditions.[157]

SUSETTE "BRIGHT EYES" LAFLESCHE TIBBLES (1854–1903) was the first of her tribe to go to the East to be educated. A teacher at the Presbyterian Mission School on the Omaha reservation had a contact at the Elizabeth Institute for Young Ladies in New Jersey, who arranged for her admission in 1869. After completing her education, Bright Eyes returned to the reservation after six years expecting to teach at the reservation school, only to be told she could not. Despite multiple attempts by bureaucrats to deny her the post, even though there were rules that preferred tribal members for teaching positions, Bright Eyes persevered. When the Omaha agent refused to give her permission to leave the reservation to take the test for her teaching certificate, she borrowed her father's fastest horse and rode to Tekamah, Nebraska, anyway. After multiple letters to the commissioner for Indian affairs and a threat to go to the newspapers with her story, she became the first Omaha teacher on the reservation.[158]

Bright Eyes's tenacity served her well when faced with the next phase of her life. In 1879, she took her first step onto the national stage when she served as interpreter for Ponca chief Standing Bear in his case against the federal government. The Ponca were relatives and neighbors to the Omaha, so it shocked and angered the Omaha when in late 1876 the government ordered the Ponca to give up their reservation in Nebraska and move to Indian Territory (present-day Oklahoma). The U.S. military responded to their defeat at the Battle of the Little Bighorn with a policy to crush the remaining plains tribes and move them to reservations. Part of this plan involved moving certain Plains tribes already on reservations, like the Ponca, to new reservations far away from their homelands.[159]

Standing Bear initially refused the relocation order but gave in

Portrait of Susette LaFlesche Tibbles by José María Mora, circa 1879. *National Portrait Gallery, Smithsonian Institution.*

when the military denied food and water to his people's winter camp. In May 1877, the military force marched the Ponca to Indian Territory. They continued to suffer in their new home. More than a third of the tribe died within the first year from malaria, including Standing Bear's only son, fourteen-year-old Bear Shield. Before Bear Shield died, he asked his father to bury him in Nebraska. So, in January 1879, Standing Bear and twenty-nine others started the five hundred mile walk back to Nebraska to fulfill his son's dying wish. They had little food, money or proper clothing for the sixty-two-day trek north through winter weather. Joseph LaFlesche's family welcomed them upon their arrival and were horrified at the signs of starvation, frostbite and illness among Standing Bear's group. It wasn't long, however, before soldiers arrived to march the Ponca to the military stockade at Fort Omaha.[160]

The fort's commander, General George Crook, took pity on Standing Bear's people and tipped off a local reporter for the *Omaha World-Herald*, Thomas Tibbles, who started to publish stories about their plight. Bright Eyes wanted to help the Ponca and was advised to write to Tibbles. Her uncle Frank LaFlesche was one of Standing Bear's group and said that the Ponca had "never signed any papers, petition or treaty to be taken down to Indian Territory." The Ponca asked to stay with the Omaha tribe or even with the Lakota, even though they had been enemies. The government denied all of their requests. The Ponca were told the Omaha would be moved to Indian Territory as well. Bright Eyes passed this information along to Tibbles.[161]

Two attorneys offered to represent Standing Bear in a suit against the government. The case centered on whether Standing Bear and all other American Indians were citizens of the United States. Throughout the trial, Bright Eyes translated the proceedings for Standing Bear, and when he stood before the court to make his plea, she stood next to him to translate his words for the judge. The court case concluded with a victory not only for the Ponca but for all Native Americans as well. Judge Elmer Dundy released Standing Bear on the principle that an Indian was a person in the eyes of the law. Standing Bear was allowed to bury his son on tribal ground. The trial also piqued the interest of eastern reformers looking for a new cause to replace abolition. They found that cause in the plight of the Native American people, and they found the ideal spokesperson in the person of Susette Bright Eyes LaFlesche. After the trial, Thomas Tibbles helped organize a speaking tour for Standing Bear along the East Coast, with Bright Eyes as his interpreter. The tour was a success and brought attention to the plight of Native Americans. Bright Eyes translated for Standing Bear but also spoke for herself. The quiet, attractive young woman impressed eastern audiences with her excellent English and Americanized dress. Susette's speaking events drew crowds and encouraged philanthropically minded people to donate money for projects on the reservations.[162]

Bright Eyes continued to give lectures and appear before government committees after the first tour with Standing Bear. In one of her speeches, she spoke out against the many injustices against American Indian tribes by the U.S. government, especially forced relocations from their homelands. She criticized the prevailing opinions about "what shall be done with the Indian?"—which were either extermination or "civilizing him"—and offered a different option:

> *We offer a solution to the Indian problem. This solution will end all wars; it will end the shedding of the blood of innocent women and children; it will stop all these wrongs which have gone on month after month, year after year, for a hundred years.*
>
> *The solution of the Indian problem, as it is called, is citizenship. Like all great questions which have agitated the world, the solution is simple—so simple that men cannot understand it. They look for something complicated, something wonderful, as the answer to a question which has puzzled the wisest heads for a hundred years.*[163]

Her lectures helped influence Helen Hunt Jackson to write *A Century of Dishonor*, which became the primary text of the American Indian reform movement in the late nineteenth century. In 1881, Susette married the recently widowed Thomas Tibbles and became stepmother to his two young daughters. The couple continued to travel and speak throughout the East and Europe. She also helped Thomas with his editorial work for newspapers and wrote essays of her own. Their efforts focused on obtaining full citizenship for Native Americans, believing that to be the foundation for all other reforms.[164]

In 1890, Thomas Tibbles returned to his job with the *Omaha World Herald*, and he and Bright Eyes traveled to the Pine Ridge Agency in South Dakota, where they were present when the U.S. cavalry massacred a group of Lakota at Wounded Knee. The event happened when the soldiers tried to disarm the Lakota and one man refused to give up his rifle. Bright Eyes was staying with a Lakota family nearby and helped terrified women and children find shelter as the battle occurred. Later, she helped tend to the wounded.[165]

In 1895, the Tibbleses moved to Lincoln, where Thomas edited *The Independent*, a Populist newspaper. Susette wrote columns for the newspaper. In 1898, she worked with Fannie Reed Griffin to produce a booklet for the Trans-Mississippi Exposition of 1898, a world's fair held in Omaha. Bright Eyes wanted to highlight the history and traditions of her people and bring greater awareness about them. She provided not only the information for the text but also sketches of Omaha men and women in their traditional attire. The booklet, *Oo-Mah-Ha Ta-Wa-Tha* (Omaha City), is considered the first book illustrated by an American Indian. It was one of the many illustrated stories that Bright Eyes would become known for. The booklet included the text of the treaty between the Omaha and the U.S. government, profiles of major Omaha chiefs, including her father, and examples of the Omaha people's folklore.[166]

The Tibbleses remained in Lincoln, although Susette also had an allotment on the Omaha Reservation near Logan Creek, where they kept another house. That is where Thomas brought his wife when she fell sick in May 1903 so that she might be closer to the land she loved and cared for by her sister Susan, a doctor. Bright Eyes died during the early morning hours of May 26, 1903, in her home on Logan Creek. After her death, she was eulogized in the U.S. Senate, where she was remembered for her activism for Native American peoples. In 1983, she was inducted into the Nebraska Hall of Fame with a bust recognizing her as a spokesperson for her people, a writer and an artist. In 1994, she was inducted into the National Women's Hall of Fame.[167]

Bust of Susette LaFlesche Tibbles, Nebraska Hall of Fame, State Capitol Building, Lincoln, Nebraska. *Courtesy of Nikolyn McDonald.*

THE SECOND LaFLESCHE SISTER, ROSALIE LaFLESCHE FARLEY (1861–1900), was the only one of Joseph LaFlesche's daughters by Mary Gale not to attend school in the East. Instead, she attended the mission and government schools on the reservation and in 1880 married Edward Farley, the son of Irish immigrants. While Susette traveled the country speaking out for Native American rights, Rosalie stayed on the reservation and continued her father's work of easing the Omaha's transition into the world of the whites.[168]

Rosalie and Ed had ten children, eight of whom survived to adulthood. Her house on the Omaha Reservation became a place for both white and Indians to gather, since she knew English well and was familiar with tribal ways. In 1881, Rosalie befriended Alice Fletcher, an ethnologist who studied many Native American tribes, including the Omaha. Alice had first worked with Bright Eyes and Thomas Tibbles on an unprecedented trip to live among the Lakota on their reservation in South Dakota. Fletcher would also have a forty-year-long working relationship with Francis LaFlesche, the LaFlesche sisters' half brother, who was also an ethnologist. Rosalie helped Alice collect information about traditional Omaha society and customs before the knowledge was lost. They became longtime friends.[169]

In 1882, Rosalie worked with her sister Bright Eyes, Thomas Tibbles and Alice Fletcher to get a law through Congress to grant the Omaha their lands in severalty. Under the Omaha Allotment Act of 1882, each Omaha man, woman and child would receive a portion of tribal land held in trust by the government for twenty-five years. The Omaha Act of 1882 was controversial, but many viewed it as a way of preventing the government from forcing the Omaha off their land like they had the Ponca. It was a precursor to the Dawes Act in 1887, which Fletcher helped enact and administered for the government. The Dawes Act distributed communally owned reservation lands to individual tribal members in allotments for individual household ownership. More significantly, upon allotment, the Indian became an American citizen. Unfortunately, both acts allowed the government to sell off any surplus lands, resulting in American Indians losing total control of reservation lands.[170]

Rosalie and Ed both taught at the mission school prior to severalty. They took their allotment as a couple near the town of Bancroft, close to other LaFlesche family members. They moved to their land in 1884 and started a cooperative grazing project, Farley Pasture. The grazing program fenced in the cattle rather than croplands, addressing the problem of wandering cattle on the reservation. Ed Farley took out a twenty-year lease on eighteen thousand acres of unallotted land. Indians could use the grazing land at no cost, while whites could do so by paying a fee.[171]

Rosalie served as de facto business manager for the family. She kept the accounts and did all the business correspondence. She managed contact with the tribe and acted as interpreter between Ed and non–English speaking tribal leaders. When there was a dispute over leases on Indian allotments, she took the matter to court. She also managed the funds donated to the tribe from Susette's lectures in the East. Rosalie was also the family correspondent, and it is because of her that the LaFlesche family papers survived. She died in 1900 at the age of thirty-nine after suffering years of poor health.[172]

The third LaFlesche sister, Marguerite LaFlesche Picotte Diddock (1862–1945), was a teacher, interpreter and the Omaha Reservation's first field matron. She attended the mission and reservation schools and then went east with her younger sister Susan to the Elizabeth Institute. Like her older sisters, she taught school upon her return to the reservation in 1882, but two years later she decided to continue her education. This time she joined two of her sisters to attend the Hampton Normal and Agricultural Institute in Virginia. There she met Charles Picotte, a half-French, half-Dakota from the Yankton Agency. They both graduated in 1887 and married the following year. The Picottes returned to the Omaha agency, where Marguerite went back to teaching and Charles managed the LaFlesche family's land until he died in 1892.[173]

In 1896, Marguerite became the first field matron on the Omaha Reservation. The Office of Indian Affairs created the Field Matron Program in 1890 to acculturate Native American women into white American society. Marguerite was a perfect candidate given her father's influence and her eastern education. It was a challenging job with mixed results even on the Omaha Reservation, where Joseph LaFlesche had long worked to encourage his people to adopt a white American lifestyle. Marguerite left the program after four years. She outlived her sisters, dying in 1945 at the age of eighty-three.[174]

Susan LaFlesche Picotte (1865–1915) was the youngest daughter of Joseph LaFlesche and Mary Gale. Susan's early life reflects the transition her people were going through in the 1860s. When she was born, the Omaha people still lived in earth lodges and tipis, alternating between growing corn and hunting buffalo. Despite being born into a very Native American way of life, she spent most of her early years in a two-story wood-frame house attending the mission or reservation school.[175]

In 1879, as their sister Bright Eyes started off for her lecture tour on the East Coast, Marguerite and Susan also traveled east, following in their older sister's footsteps to attend the Elizabeth Institute. Both girls graduated and returned to the reservation in 1882. Like her sisters before her, Susan took a teaching position. In her case, it was at the newly reopened Presbyterian Mission School. She taught at the mission school for two years before Alice Fletcher urged her to attend the Hampton Normal and Agricultural Institute in Virginia to further her education. Susan, Marguerite, their half sister Lucy and Lucy's husband all left to attend the Institute in August 1884.[176]

The Hampton Normal and Agricultural Institute opened in 1868 under the direction of Samuel Chapman Armstrong, a former U.S. army general. It started as a school for African Americans, both former slaves and free, to transform them into teachers, homemakers, farmers and tradesmen. One of the Institute's most celebrated graduates was Booker T. Washington, who went on to form the Tuskegee Institute in Alabama. In 1878, the Hampton Institute expanded its student base when it accepted a group for American Indian men and women. Seventeen of these students were former prisoners and suspected ringleaders from the Red River War. Captain Richard Henry Pratt, who later formed the Carlisle Indian Industrial School in Pennsylvania, oversaw the prisoners at Fort Marion in Florida and taught them English. He convinced them to continue their education at Hampton, as there was no other school for them at the time.[177]

When Susan arrived at the Hampton Institute, there were 659 students, with one-sixth of them from different Native American tribes. Of the American Indian students, just under half were girls. The school's purpose was primarily to train teachers, with the idea that they would return to their homes to instruct others. In many respects, Susan was the perfect student for the Hampton Institute. She already embodied much of what the Institute was trying to accomplish: she was fluent in English as well as five Native languages, she had grown up in a community that was already trying to adopt a white lifestyle, she was a devout Christian and had already spent three years in an East Coast city absorbing white American culture. While at Hampton, she joined the temperance group, the Christian Endeavor Society and the Lend a Hand Club. She also visited the poor and the sick.[178]

Susan graduated from the Hampton Institute as salutatorian on May 20, 1886. In her graduation speech, "My Childhood and Womanhood," she echoed her father:

> We who are educated have to be pioneers of Indian civilization. We have to prepare our people to live in the white man's way, to use the white man's books, and to use his laws if you will only give them to us. The white people have reached a high standard of civilization, but how many years has it taken them? We are only beginning; so do not try to put us down, but help us to climb higher. Give us a chance.[179]

A chance was also something Susan still wanted—specifically, a chance to further her education to become a doctor.

Susan's desire to attend medical school set her apart. There were few women doctors in the late nineteenth century, let alone Native American doctors, yet she had considerable support for her endeavor. General Armstrong, the founder of the Hampton Institute, and the school's physician, Dr. Martha M. Waldron, supported Susan's desire to enter medical school. Waldron directed Susan to the Woman's Medical College of Pennsylvania to continue her studies. The only issue was funding. Susan did not win a full scholarship, and with time running out to enroll, she sought Alice Fletcher's help. Alice in turn enlisted her friend Sara Kinney, who had connections to activists on the East Coast. In the end, a combination of donations from the Connecticut Indian Association and a government stipend for American Indian students made it possible for Susan to pursue her dream. Susan thanked her "many mothers" in the association who supported her education. Susan wrote to Sara Kinney, saying, "It has always been a desire of mine to study medicine ever since I was a small girl.…For even then I saw the needs of my people for a good physician." She also shared her intent to instruct the women of her tribe about cleanliness, cooking, nursing and housekeeping.[180]

After her second year of medical school, Susan returned home to the Omaha Reservation for the summer. While there she got firsthand experience of what it would be like serving as a doctor on the reservation when she helped care for the sick through a measles epidemic, including Rosalie and one of her children. The experience solidified Susan's determination to complete her studies. She wrote to Sara Kinney:

> I only can say, I want to do so much because there is so much to be done. I can only say to you, I shall try and do my best, try to aid them not only

physically but mentally and morally. I may be too ambitious but I have to help My Heavenly Father, as well as the remembrance that my own father who has worked all his life long for my people last left his children expecting them to carry on his work.[181]

Susan graduated with a MD in 1889, first in her class of thirty-six and the first Native American woman to earn a medical degree. She then interned at the Woman's Hospital for four months, after a brief vacation of multiple speaking engagements in branches of the Connecticut Indian Association and a quick trip home. After her internship, she returned to the reservation as physician for the government school, but it wasn't long until her responsibilities extended to the whole tribe.[182]

Before returning home, Susan had written to the Commissioner of Indian Affairs asking to be appointed government physician at the Omaha Agency boarding school in Macy, where her sister Marguerite was head teacher. The commissioner agreed. While the government had only hired her to tend the students at the school, it didn't take long for the adults to be asking for "Dr. Susan," rather than the white doctor. Within three months, she had taken over most of the other doctor's patients and she officially took his place when he left abruptly. At twenty-four years of age, she was now responsible for the 1,244 Omaha scattered across 1,350 square miles of the reservation.[183]

Transportation was her biggest problem at the beginning. The roads on the reservation were poor. If the patient was close, she walked. If not, she rode her buckskin horse. Horseback riding wasn't conducive to preserving her bottles and thermometers, so she began hiring a team of horses or people brought patients to her. Eventually, she had to buy her own buggy. Her office hours were all hours of day and night ,and she often started work at seven o'clock in the morning and ended at ten at night. During the first winter, she faced two epidemics of influenza. She also treated dysentery, cholera and conjunctivitis, often trying to teach her patients hygienic habits as part of the treatment process. Over one winter, she saw over six hundred patients. The work was exhausting, but she loved it. She wrote after her second year: "I am enjoying my work exceedingly, and feel more interest in, and more attached to my people than ever before."[184]

The community also came to Susan for matters beyond their health. People asked her advice on everything from business and financial matters, legal questions and politics to personal dilemmas and marital advice. Susan and Marguerite were active in the Presbyterian church, attending Sunday services, singing and interpreting the service into the Omaha language. They were back on Sunday evenings for Christian Endeavor meetings with the young people and again on Wednesday evenings for prayer meetings. Neither Susan nor Marguerite was shy in sharing their thoughts on issues. They encouraged young couples to get marriage licenses and marry in the church. As more Omaha were holding Christian burials, the sisters helped with funerals as well. Susan was also heavily involved with the students at the boarding school. She gave them lectures about the importance of good hygiene. They also played games and had sing-alongs. Susan also started a reading room for the children with help from the Connecticut Indian Association.[185]

By the fall of 1892, the pace of her work had caught up with her. Her own health began to suffer. She fell ill and became bedridden for weeks. Susan had been plagued with recurring health issues since medical school but assumed it was just stress. She finally recovered enough by the new year to return to work, but that spring she took a hard fall from her buggy that once again forced her to suspend work until she recovered. Finally, in the fall of 1893, her illness returned. Pain in her neck and ears forced her to spend much of her time with her mother, who was critically ill and lonely. With none of her sisters available to care for the frail woman, she resigned her position as government physician and joined her mother at her home on Logan Creek. Rosalie wrote to their brother Francis: "She said it was going to be hard for her as she loved her work and hated to give it up but she felt it ought to be done for mother, and she knew she would never regret it."[186]

While her career now seemed less of a concern, Susan surprised everyone in 1894 by marrying Henry Picotte, brother of her sister Marguerite's first husband. In many respects he wasn't like Susan: he was only semiliterate, and he didn't abstain from alcohol. He had also performed in a Wild West show. Many were concerned, if not angry, about the marriage. In the late nineteenth century, marriage meant the end of any career that a woman had, but Susan didn't let marriage stop her. She and her new husband settled in Bancroft, where she continued to serve both Indians and whites. There they laid out an orchard and garden and Susan made space for her office in their new home, resuming her medical career. Whether at her house in Bancroft or at her mother's farm, Susan always placed a lighted lantern in the window so that people needing medical attention could find her. No longer the government physician, she had more time to participate in tribal life while still taking care of patients. She and Marguerite became increasingly close.

I shall always fight good and hard even if I have to fight alone.

Susan La Flesche Picotte, M.D.

Susan LaFlesche Picotte statue, Centennial Mall, Lincoln, Nebraska. *Courtesy of Nikolyn McDonald.*

In 1895, Marguerite remarried to Walter Diddock, a white man who taught at the school. The sisters continued to work together in the community, and each had their first child within a few months of each other.[187]

Susan had two children, Caryl Henry and Pierre. As a mother, Susan struggled to balance her career and her family, largely because her patients wouldn't let her give up working. They wanted her and no one else. When Caryl and Pierre were babies, Susan often ended up taking them with her when she visited patients. Support from her husband and the help of nearby friends to watch her children made it possible for her to continue working. But in 1905, her husband died from complications due to drinking. Susan was left with an invalid mother and two young sons to care for.[188]

After her husband's death, the Presbyterian Board of Home Missions appointed Susan as a missionary to her tribe. She was the first American Indian to hold such a position. It also provided a small stipend to help the family get by. As a missionary, she was both pastor, janitor, organist and Sunday school clerk for the church. She conducted services in the Omaha language to attract more people. Her missionary work was successful: twenty Omaha children and twenty adults were baptized in one day in December 1907. Three days later, fifteen more people were baptized. The *Walthill Times* noted, "This is not the result of a revival but is the culmination of the mission work of Dr. Susan La F. Picotte."[189]

In the fall of 1906, Susan was the only woman and only Omaha Indian who bought a lot in the new railroad town of Walthill on the Omaha Reservation. She sold her husband's allotment in South Dakota and leased her own 640-acre allotment to finance the purchase. Marguerite's husband also bought a lot, so the sisters continued to live close to each other. Susan built a new, modern home in Walthill. It had a furnace and indoor bathroom, as well as plenty of windows for light and fresh air. She continued her work as a missionary, serving two churches now, and as a physician. She and Marguerite continued their work in the community as well. Susan was president of the Missionary Society and served for three years as chair of the Nebraska Federation of Women's Clubs. She and Marguerite were charter members of a new chapter of Eastern Star, a Christian service-based organization. The two sisters participated in local community projects such as lectures, concerts, fundraisers and the county fair. They also took part in Sunday school conventions and University of Nebraska Extension service agricultural meetings. They even started a small library.[190]

In Walthill, Susan continued her mission to improve the health and hygiene of her people. She helped start the Thurston County Medical Society and was a member of the Walthill Health Board and the Nebraska State Medical Society. She was a temperance advocate after seeing the effects of alcoholism during medical school and witnessing the effects firsthand again with her husband. Her father had organized a police force in 1856 that successfully combated the use of alcohol on the reservation until his death in 1888. Since that time, however, there had been little to no enforcement of prohibition laws on the reservation, bootleggers abounded and alcoholism plagued the tribe. When called as an expert witness in an inquest where a man died from drinking, she said:

> *We find the Omaha Indian before the advent of the white man a fine specimen of manhood, physically and morally of good health;…[but] with liquor, we find these conditions radically changed and reversed. We find physical degeneration of the Indian.*[191]

Susan campaigned against alcohol on the reservation, writing letters and lobbying legislative bodies to leading a voting campaign and collaborating with the Omaha Tribal Council to establish a tribal police force. Unfortunately, it was not an issue that the law seemed able to control.[192]

With everything else failing, Susan began her own temperance movement. She spoke at churches, schools and local communities. Soon, her speeches and newspaper articles went beyond just banning alcohol to other issues of public health, such as the communal drinking cup, keeping out flies and not congregating in enclosed homes, all of which helped prevent the spread of disease. She asked the Omaha people to focus on preventing disease so that they wouldn't need her services as a doctor. Like Harriet MacMurphy (chapter 4), she used women's clubs to pressure for legislation. She used her role as chair of the State Health Committee of the Nebraska Federation of Women's Clubs to get a state law passed banning communal cups. Susan also worked to educate the Omaha people about tuberculosis and how to avoid the deadly disease. She suggested that lectures about tuberculosis, communal drinking cups and fly eradication should be given in all Indian schools. She also recommended monthly tuberculosis testing of children in boarding schools to prevent rapid spread of the disease. When the commissioner of Indian affairs did not respond to her request, she took it upon herself to screen every student in the Walthill schools for free.[193]

Susan's biggest dream for her tribe was to build a hospital on the reservation. As always, the issue was raising the money. Attempts to raise money by both the Connecticut Indian Association and an order of sisters from the Catholic Church failed. With these failures, Susan did what she often did, start a letter-writing campaign. She also spoke wherever she could and used the local newspaper to build interest. Then she contacted the Presbyterian Board of Home Missions. The board committed $8,000 while the Religious Society of Friends in Massachusetts donated another $500. Another $100 came from a benefit concert held in Philadelphia. A Presbyterian church in Sioux City and an organization in Omaha each offered to equip and furnish a room in the hospital. Assistance poured in from people and organizations around the area, including Marguerite and her husband, who donated the land.[194]

In January 1913, Susan realized her dream of having a hospital near her patients. The *Walthill Times* reported on the event and described the new building:

> *The hospital stands on a prominent elevation in the northwest part of the town and its massive architectural lines, of the mission type, produce an imposing landscape feature overlooking the village....A full sized basement contains the heating plant, kitchen, dining room and housekeepers quarters....*
>
> *The hospital proper has two general wards, each with a capacity of six beds, five private wards, obstetrics room, operating room, diet kitchen, two bath rooms, linen closet, infants room and the reception room or office.*[195]

The article also described how the building was very modern, with "steam heat, city water and electric lights." Susan and Marguerite furnished the Joseph LaFlesche Operating Room in honor of their father.[196]

Susan enjoyed her efforts for only two years. The illness that had long plagued her grew worse. The disease ate away at the bones of her inner ear, eventually causing hearing loss. It also caused considerable pain in her neck and back. In 1914, doctors diagnosed her with "decay of the bone." It was probably cancer. By early 1915, it had spread into the bones of her face. She had two operations, but they could not prevent the inevitable. Marguerite and her husband went so far to reach out to Marie Curie in France because of her promotion of radium as a potential cancer cure. They told Curie about Susan, and soon a package arrived from Paris containing a radium

Susan LaFlesche Picotte Center (formerly hospital), Walthill, Nebraska. *Courtesy of Nikolyn McDonald.*

pellet in a lead-lined box, but it was too late. Susan died at 1:00 a.m. on September 18, 1915.[197]

A week after her death, Susan's friend and village attorney Harry Keefe summed up her life eloquently:

> *We are confronted here with a character rising to greatness and to great deeds out of conditions which seldom produce more than mediocre men and women, achieving great and beneficent ends over obstacles almost insurmountable. In her death the Indians lose their best and truest friend; the community and the state sustains an irreparable loss; and there is ended one of the most fruitful, unselfish and useful lives.*[198]

Following her death, the Presbyterian Home Mission Board renamed the Walthill Hospital in her honor as the Dr. Susan Picotte Memorial Hospital. The building still stands today. It was placed on the National Register of Historic Places in 1988 and named a National Historic Landmark in 1993. It is currently being renovated into the Susan LaFlesche Picotte Center and will have a museum, a wellness clinic, mental health services and a youth programming room.[199]

The LaFlesche sisters of the Umo^{n}ho^n tribe exemplified the resilience, leadership and dedication needed to navigate and advocate for their people during a period of intense change and hardship. Through their various roles as educators, activists and cultural preservers, they not only advanced the rights and recognition of Native Americans but also bridged the gap between Indigenous and Western cultures. Their legacy continues to inspire and remind us of the critical importance of education, advocacy and cultural preservation in the fight for justice and equality.

7
EDUCATOR AND ATHLETE

LOUISE POUND

The University of Nebraska provided an inclusive educational environment from its start, allowing both men and women to attend. Among its early students was Louise Pound, a remarkable scholar and advocate for women's education and professional advancement. Over her fifty-year tenure at the University, Pound distinguished herself in as a scholar of philology and folklore while advocating for women in academia. Pound's significance extends beyond the classroom as well. She was a celebrated athlete and a key figure in the "New Woman" movement, which championed women's pursuit of education and careers traditionally dominated by men.

Nebraska, like other states with land-grant colleges, gave women an opportunity to earn a college degree. While many women graduates in the late nineteenth and early twentieth centuries became teachers, about 15 percent entered other professions, such as medicine, journalism and the law.[200] The Morrill Land Grant Act of 1862 created nearly one hundred tuition-free colleges and universities, most of them in the West. The government left it to the states to decide whether they would allow both men and women at their colleges. Although some were concerned about allowing women to attend the same classes as men, pragmatism typically won out. The West needed professionals, especially teachers, so many states opened coed campuses.[201]

The University of Nebraska, founded in 1869, was one of the many land-grant colleges created under the Morrill Act. From its opening, the university committed to educating women, allowing them to attend the same classes as male students. The first class had 130 students, 110 of which were enrolled in the university's preparatory school. There was one woman in the first-year class of 5, and 6 women were irregular college students. By the 1890s, the University of Nebraska had the first graduate program west of the Mississippi River, and by 1898, only three other state universities had larger graduate student enrollment than Nebraska.[202]

LOUISE POUND (1872–1958) was one of the University of Nebraska's first graduate students and served as a faculty member for over fifty years. She has been described as an international scholar, educator, author, editor, folklorist, athlete and authority on the American language. She was also part of the "New Woman" movement, which appeared in the late nineteenth and early twentieth centuries. These women sought self-fulfillment through education and careers, often entering fields dominated by men. Louise's accomplishments in sports and scholarship made her a notable figure in this movement.[203]

A western educational institution with treeless surrounding, 1899, Nebraska. *National Archives and Records Administration, NAID: 7029139.*

An example of a one-room schoolhouse, common in early Nebraska. Cunningham School, Pioneers Park, Lincoln, Nebraska. *Author's collection.*

Louise, who was an extraordinary person in her own right, came from an equally accomplished family. Her father, Stephen Pound, was a prominent attorney and judge. Within a year of settling in Lincoln in 1869, Stephen was a probate judge. He later served in the Nebraska legislature in 1872–73 and was a member of the 1875 state constitutional convention. In 1876, he won election as a district judge and held that position for twelve years before returning to his law practice.[204] In many ways, Louise's mother, Laura Pound, was a New Woman before the concept even existed. Not only did she tend to domestic duties, including educating her three children, but she also served the community and pursued her own educational interests. She helped create the first public library in Lincoln and the Lincoln chapter of the Daughters of the American Revolution, which maintained the Antelope Park Botanical Garden and a memorial fountain. She was a charter member of the Hayden Art Club, which supported the Art Department at the University of Nebraska (see chapter 8) and the Lincoln Woman's Club, where she headed the Woman's Club Science Department. On top of all these activities, she attended language classes at the university.[205]

Louise's siblings were also quite accomplished. Her older brother, Roscoe, received a PhD in botany and then went to law school. Eventually, he became dean of Harvard's law school and advocated revising laws to reflect social change. Louise's younger sister, Olivia, became a teacher and became dean of girls and assistant principal at Lincoln's high school. While there she developed a vocational counseling department and helped needy female pupils, often inviting them to stay at the Pound home while they completed their education.[206]

The Pounds ignored prevailing beliefs at the time about educating girls. Instead, all three children learned sciences and mathematics and played sports. Louise was first known in Lincoln because of her athletic achievements, rather than her academic success. She played tennis and basketball and cycled. She also taught herself how to figure skate and ski. Louise had a competitive nature that she showed in many sports over the years.[207] Her favorite sport was tennis, which she taught herself to play after becoming bored with the more common game of lawn croquet. Tennis was a new sport in the United States in the 1880s, played by both women and men. Louise was renowned in Lincoln for her skill on the court and became the first female member of the Lincoln Tennis Club. She was the club's only female member through the 1890s. At the age of eighteen, Louise became the Lincoln City Tennis Champion. She won tennis titles at both the University of Nebraska and the University of Chicago, often over male opponents. Her greatest achievement in tennis was becoming the Women's Western Tennis Champion in 1897. After that win, she wrote to her parents, "I've made a name for myself now and have won a prize and am content." In 1900, while attending the University of Heidelberg, she won the city championship there as well.[208]

Sports would be a lifelong element of Louise's life. In her early days as a professor, she played with and coached the University of Nebraska women's basketball team. During her tenure as coach, the team never lost a game. She also helped write and publish rules for women's basketball at the university. In 1917, the University of Nebraska Women's Athletic Association awarded her a life membership out of respect for her athletic achievements. In her later years, she replaced tennis with golf, becoming a local champion, and in 1955, she became the first woman named by the *Lincoln Journal Star* to the Nebraska Athletic Hall of Fame for her accomplishments in sports.[209]

As much as Louise loved sports, she never pursued athletics professionally. Instead, she devoted herself to learning and scholarship. She viewed scholarship as a mission. She once told a friend considering an academic career that scholarship "needs many workers. If you can add just one cubic centimeter to the mass achievement of scholarship, you have not lived in vain."[210] She enrolled in the two-year preparatory program at the University of Nebraska–Lincoln at the age of fourteen. At the time, it was the only path to a college education, since there were no established high schools. In 1888, at the age of sixteen, she became a university student.[211]

Ever the overachiever, Louise was extremely active while at university. She was involved in literary societies; wrote stories, plays and poems; contributed articles to the local newspaper; and started a literary journal, *The Lasso*, with her friend Willa Cather (chapter 9). She even formed a short-lived women's military drill team. Pound did all of this while studying for dual degrees in music and English philology.[212] She graduated in 1892 as one of the first two students to receive a music diploma from the University of Nebraska. At the music department's commencement, she performed all movements of Beethoven's "Sonata Pathetique," Opus 13, No. 8; Chopin's polonaise, Opus 26, No. 2; and Rubinstein's "Le Bal." She was also the top student in her class, was class poet and orator and gave the class oration at commencement, a speech titled "Apotheosis of the Common" that criticized the prevalence of commonness in contemporary society. Louise believed in

Postcard of Main Building, State University, Lincoln, Nebraska. *J.C. & G.E. Orcutt.*

acknowledging individual achievement, unsurprising given her wide-ranging personal accomplishments.[213]

After graduation, Louise pursued her master's degree while working as a theme reader in the English Department at the University of Nebraska. The dean of the College of Arts and Sciences encouraged her to get her doctorate degree, assuring her of a position. She continued her studies at the University of Chicago during the summers of 1897–98, but she was not sure about getting her PhD there. While women were earning college undergraduate degrees around the turn of the nineteenth century, it was still rare for them to pursue higher degrees. Society still expected them to eventually marry and remain in the home.[214]

Pound, however, was a "New Woman," whether she identified as one or not. The concept of the New Woman began in the 1890s and lasted until the 1920s. New Women ignored the gender restrictions of earlier generations to pursue work outside the home in fields typically dominated by men. They chose education and career over family. According to one scholar, 40 to 60 percent of female college graduates never married because it meant leaving their chosen profession. At that time, women were led to believe they had to make a choice between a career or a family, despite the few women who managed to do both. Like other New Women, Louise committed herself to teaching, research, writing and her parents and sister, rather than devoting her life to a husband, household and children.[215]

It was popular to pursue graduate degrees in English from German universities at the time Louise was considering where to get her doctorate degree, so she chose the University of Heidelberg. She set an ambitious goal for herself, not wanting to be away from home any longer than she had to. She set out to complete her degree in one year instead of the usual two. For her specialty, she chose the field of philology—the structure, historical development and relationships of languages. Despite having to learn the German language and the distractions of an active social life, Louise persevered and completed her goal. Years later, she asserted, "Winning that degree in two semesters was the hardest thing I ever did." Her advisor liked her dissertation so much that he wanted to publish it in a philological series.[216]

After completing her dissertation at Heidelberg in 1900, Louise returned home to start a faculty position at the University of Nebraska in Lincoln. It was a position she would hold for over fifty years. She started her teaching career with a course in the Anglo-Saxon language. Over the years, she taught undergraduate literature courses and graduate classes on Anglo-Saxon,

Middle English, history of the English language and Germanic philology. She also taught seminars in her specialty areas of American English, folklore and folk song. A former student wrote of her classes: "Her interpretation of the History of English Literature made that subject a warm, living experience rather than a mere panorama of writers, periods, and dates."[217]

Her initial academic research examined word derivations in American speech patterns. Rather than looking at the speech patterns of regional areas, she and her students examined the speech habits of the entire United States. Her most significant contribution to the field of philology was questioning the supremacy of British English over American English. She believed that the two languages were distinct, that they would continue to diverge and that they should be treated individually. Her work in this area brought her to the attention of H.L. Mencken, a journalist and fellow scholar of American English. Because of their efforts, including Pound's work supporting Mencken's publication *American Language*, American English now stands on its own. [218]

Louise's interest in American English led to an interest in folklore and folk songs. In her 1921 book *Poetic Origins and the Ballad*, she challenged the prevailing theory of the communal origin of ballads with examples of ballads originating by individuals. Through this book, Louise established herself as a leading expert in her field, and her theory eventually won out. She viewed folklore as a window to the past. She wrote:

> *The folksongs and dances are not only valuable for themselves, but they make the past of each region of America very real indeed. The festival is the best way I know to acquaint people with the authentic culture of old American, and its survival in many regions.*[219]

Louise was especially interested in the customs and folklore of Nebraska. In 1916, she published a collection of folk songs from Nebraska and the middle West titled *Folksong of Nebraska and the Central West*. Her last book, *Nebraska Folklore*, published posthumously in 1959, is still the only work published on the subject. Louise loved Nebraska and encouraged local writers to write about what they knew, including one of her students, Mari Sandoz (chapter 9).[220]

In all, Louise Pound authored around two hundred articles and books in the fields of linguistics, literature, education and folklore. She co-founded the journal *American Speech* in 1925. She was a member of the American Dialect Society, American Folklore Society, National Council of Teachers of English, Nebraska State Teachers Association, American Association of University Professors and Nebraska Academy of Sciences. In 1927, she received a prestigious appointment as a delegate to the International Council on English held in London at the Royal Society of Literature. She was the only woman on the council.[221]

Louise also had a long relationship with the Modern Language Association. She joined in 1906 and held various offices, served on committees and presented papers throughout her teaching career. In 1916, she served as vice-president and as an executive committee member. But it wasn't until 1955, nine years after she had retired from teaching, that the association elected her as its first woman president.[222]

Besides teaching at the University of Nebraska, Pound lectured at the University of California–Berkeley, the Yale Linguistic Institute, the University of Chicago, Columbia and Stanford. Even though many other institutions would have hired her, she never considered leaving Nebraska. As she told a local newspaper in 1945:

> *Why should I have gone elsewhere?…To be sure, I should have had several thousand dollars more. But I could not have taken my mother, my sister, or my friends with me. I could not have lived in our 50-year-old Pound home. Instead, I should have had an apartment, or rather, two. I'd need one for my books alone. And, I'd have been just another professor. As it was, I had the experiences of teaching in various places, yet all the pleasures of staying at home with my relatives.*[223]

As a teacher, Pound was extremely supportive of her students. One former student noted how she followed the careers of her students after graduation and "was intensely proud of the 'Louise Pound alumni association,' as some of us alumni and alumnae dubbed it." She prepared her students well, many finding it easier to find jobs in academia after working with her. Pound also took an interest in students outside the classroom, especially young women whom she felt needed additional encouragement. She would often take female students out for breakfast or movies or invite them to the home she shared with her mother and sister. Having been active in clubs as a student, it was no surprise that she also took part in informal clubs with students at the university, many of them literary. Any time students needed a professor to back a non-academic group, "Miss Pound," as she preferred to be called, was likely to help them out. One notable group was the Golden Fleece, a club exclusively for redheads. This group started when three redheaded female students approached Louise, a redhead herself, about organizing a club. Miss Pound gladly obliged them.[224]

Louise also supported other professional women. She was a member of the Wooden Spoon Society, a women's group that promoted the acceptance of women in business or professional work. From 1906 to 1908 she served as director of the Nebraska chapter of the American Association of University Women, which provided financial aid to women pursuing advanced degrees, and was a member of their national council in 1913. She continued to serve the group in various roles until her retirement and left money for fellowships through the organization in her will.[225]

Louise championed fellow women academics, often sacrificing her own career advancement. Mamie Meredith, a former student and later colleague, noted, "There are others besides myself, who probably wouldn't have found it bearable to remain here if Louise Pound hadn't stayed here to champion just causes, whether popular or unpopular."[226] In the entire fifty years she worked for the University of Nebraska, she was never head of the English department. Instead, administrators would look elsewhere before promoting her. In 1920, she wrote an article titled "The College Woman and Research," in which she stated:

> *The customary explanation when women graduate students do brilliant work, better work sometimes than their male associates, is that they must be "selected women" the "few best," while their male co-workers are not a selected lass, choosing their line of work because of a special bent for it, but are in the work by chance. When a man does well, it is taken for granted that he is typical. When a woman does well, (so strong is the tradition), it is still thought to need explanation; and it is taken for granted that she is not typical but the product of special circumstances.*[227]

It is hard to argue, however, that Louise herself was not special. Throughout her life, she showed a quick mind, a competitive spirit and the determination to persevere. Her success, however, in no way diminishes the obstacles that she and other women academics had to overcome during the early twentieth century.

Toward the end of her life, Louise received many accolades. In 1940, the Women's Centennial Congress honored her as one of four University of Nebraska graduates cited as "women of distinction." She was the only one of the four who had remained in Nebraska. She also received the Distinguished Service Medal from the Kiwanis Club of Lincoln in 1947;

recognition as Distinguished Alumni by the University Alumni and Regents in 1948; and the Special Alumnae Achievement Award from Kappa Kappa Gamma in 1951.[228]

Louise announced her retirement from the University of Nebraska in June 1945. She and her sister remained in their family home and continued to support young women in the community. She died from a heart attack on June 28, 1958, a few days short of her eighty-sixth birthday, and was buried in Wyuka Cemetery in Lincoln. [229]

Louise Pound stands in the history of Nebraska women as a central figure, not only for her significant academic contributions and athletic achievements but also for her steadfast support of her students and advocacy for women's professional advancement. Her legacy as an extraordinary educator and a pioneer of the New Woman movement underscores the profound effect she had on her community and beyond. Despite facing significant gender-based challenges, Louise's perseverance and achievements paved the way for future generations of women scholars. Her enduring influence is evident in the lasting recognition of her work and the many accolades she received throughout her life.

8

GREAT PLAINS ARTIST

ELIZABETH DOLAN

S everal talented women helped shape the artistic landscape of Nebraska, one of the most notable being Elizabeth Honor Dolan (1875–1948). Unlike many of her contemporaries who had to leave Nebraska to pursue their careers, Dolan's legacy is still visible in multiple locations around Lincoln. Her pursuit of art was made possible in part by women who championed the art department at the University of Nebraska. The experiences of these women are a testament to their passion and determination for the arts in Nebraska.

Elizabeth Dolan came from humble beginnings. She was one of six children born to Irish immigrants in Fort Dodge, Iowa. Her family moved to Tecumseh, Nebraska, when she was a baby and then later settled in Lincoln. Dolan's first art classes were at the University of Nebraska School of Fine Arts, where she enrolled in 1899. Women were instrumental in early art education in Nebraska. Colleges in the state gave young women the opportunity to teach art in institutions of higher learning. Art departments were often less financially secure, resulting in men pursuing teaching positions in other fields. The University of Nebraska established a School of Fine Arts in 1885. The first three heads of the art department were women: Sarah Wool Moore, Cora Parker and Sarah Hayden.[230]

Moore, Parker and Hayden were not born in Nebraska, and each of them lived in the state for only a few years while teaching at the university. Nevertheless, they each had a significant influence on the university's art program. Born in Plattsburg, New York, SARAH WOOL MOORE (1846–1911) graduated from the Packer Collegiate Institute in 1865. She taught for a few years before traveling through Europe, where she spent five years learning painting in Vienna. She arrived at the University of Nebraska in 1884, where she taught painting, drawing and art history and later became head of the art department. As department head, she advocated with the university's regents to improve the art program. She wrote letters to the regents asking that they keep course fees low to attract students and make teacher's stipends respectable to recruit and keep staff. She also asked for funds to add an art library and a new art studio with plaster casts of classical sculpture used for drawing exercises. Moore's efforts increased the class sizes in the university's art program.[231]

Moore also organized the Haydon Art Club in 1888. This organization later became the Nebraska Art Association, the support organization for the Sheldon Memorial Art Gallery on the University of Nebraska Lincoln campus. Moore has the distinction of designing the seal adopted by the Nebraska Historical Society. She resigned in 1892 and returned to the East Coast.[232]

CORA PARKER (1859–1944) succeeded Moore as head of the art department. Parker had degrees from the Cincinnati Art School and the Julian Academy in Paris. Her tenure as director of the university's art department became increasingly challenging. In 1897, the university considered creating a School of Art, but the director of the School of Music refused to direct both schools without a pay increase. The art department continued, but the university didn't fund it. Instead, the department had to turn to the Haydon Art Club for financial support. Parker's salary came from a combination of money from the Art Club treasury and part from a five-dollar fee charged to each student. Parker resigned in 1899 in protest over potential closure of the art department. In the end, the regents kept the department after all and offered Sarah Hayden the position of director. Cora Parker returned to the East to work for the Bruce Art Museum in Greenwich, Connecticut.[233]

SARAH SEWELL HAYDEN (1862–1939) already had considerable experience and accolades when one of her instructors in Chicago suggested she apply to be art department director at the University of Nebraska. She had taught at several institutions, spent two winters in Paris, received a silver medal from the Chicago Art Institute and had her work accepted at the Paris Salon. The university offered her the post in 1899. Hayden benefited from an improving interest in the arts in Nebraska. She remained with the university as director for seventeen years, resigning in 1916. It was during her tenure that the Haydon Art Club became the Nebraska Art Association (NAA). It was under the teaching of Sarah Hayden that Elizabeth Dolan started her art education.[234]

Dolan attended courses in the School of Fine Arts in 1891–92 and in 1894–95, but it wasn't until seventeen years later, in 1912, that she fully pursued her dream of becoming an artist by enrolling in the Chicago Institute of Art. At that point, she was forty-one years of age. She later said that 1912 was the year of her artistic birth:

> *October, 1912, life opened. Stepping off the train in Chicago, I faced a new world and a new life eagerly. My real life began when I entered the Chicago Art Institute enrolled as a student. Beyond that time I have only vague memories of unhappiness, unfruitful struggles to receive an art education in my effort to become a famous painter.*[235]

She received two scholarships to attend the Chicago Institute of Art, and the director of the school noted that she was the most talented pupil at the school during that time.[236]

After graduating from the Art Institute in 1914, she enrolled at the Art Students League in New York City, where she studied for four years. She stayed in New York City painting landscapes, miniatures and portraits and designing stained-glass windows for Louis Tiffany until 1925, when she sailed for Paris to enter the École des Beaux-Arts at Fontainebleau. Fontainebleau was the only school in the world that taught frescoing, and Dolan was the only one in her class of twenty-five to graduate with a diploma in that art form. She also received a diploma in painting.[237]

An illness in her family forced Dolan to return to Nebraska after her graduation from Fontainebleau. Fortunately, she found an opportunity to use her talents to paint murals at a new natural history museum that was being built on the University of Nebraska–Lincoln campus. Morrill Hall featured the state's fossil collection, and museum director Dr. E.H. Barbour hired Dolan as a "decorator" for one hundred dollars a week to paint background murals for the fossil displays. She signed a contract in 1927 and traveled to western Nebraska to make sketches of two famous fossil-bed hills in Sioux County and other sites in Dawes and Brown Counties. Through this project, she built her reputation as a muralist. Her murals appeared all over the museum and bore her signature, including murals on the east and west walls of the main hall, a mural on the north

Portrait of Elizabeth Dolan seated with paint easel and brush. *Nebraska State Historical Society Photograph Collections.*

wall above the museum entrance depicting the life of a Cro-Magnon man and the fossil exhibits along the corridors of the first floor. These murals were large, one as big as sixteen feet high and seventy feet wide and another measuring nine feet high and seventy-five feet wide. She also painted several habitat backgrounds on the lower level of the museum.[238] In 1928, even before the murals were finished, the *Morning World-Herald* was proclaiming her success:

> *It looks as if the midwest had produced another genius in the person of Elizabeth Honor Dolan, formerly of Lincoln and later of New York city, the artist who is making the mural decorations in Morrill Hall on the University of Nebraska campus. There is not much doubt but what these murals will one day be acclaimed as one of America's outstanding achievements in the world of art.*[239]

The newspaper further heralded Dolan's reputation in the art world. They reported that the editor of *The American Magazine of Art* had written:

> *The reception in Morrill Hall also introduced to those from afar some exceptionally fine paintings made by Miss Dolan for habitat groups set forth on the first floor of this building in the museum department. These paintings not only compare in quality with the best of the kind that have been done in our eastern museums, but in some respects are superior. They are in high key, to an extent imaginative and yet entirely accurate and effective. The rendering is broad and effective.*[240]

Dolan's murals were so astounding that many stopped to watch her paint. She told a reporter for the *Daily Nebraskan* that "the students are my greatest bother....It is so distracting to try to paint when people are watching you and making remarks." She tried to put up signs and canvases for privacy, but they were torn down or ignored. Dr. Barbour wrote in a letter to C.H. Morrill:

> *We have but one problem and that is the problem of visitors. We will never be able to settle that for the place is becoming too well known....Poor Miss Dolan who is so nearly done that she is trying conscientiously to finish has pinned on her back a big placard, to the effect that she would like to have her friends give her a chance to do her work.*[241]

Dolan's murals for the museum used an illustrative approach, using outlines and colors to suggest the forms of trees, rocks and animals in the background, giving them the feel of a watercolor. A reporter described seeing her work for the first time as experiencing "a peculiar sensation difficult to express, but very real." The murals transported visitors to the museum to another world, "a strangely luminous; a new world, very young and very beautiful, unscarred and sinless." Dolan had presented an illusion: "She has effaced eons and has envisioned for us a strange eery [sic] world flooded with a light that was never on land or sea."[242] The university was so pleased with her work that they later commissioned her to paint portraits of C.H. Morrill and his wife; Dr. Samuel Avery, a former UNL chancellor; and Dr. E.H. Barbour for the Founder's Hall of the museum.[243]

Prairie Woman, by Elizabeth Dolan. Attorney General's Office, State Capitol Building, Lincoln, Nebraska. *Courtesy of Nikolyn McDonald.*

Dolan's next achievement was in 1930 when the state commissioned her to paint a mural for the new state capitol building. Appearing in the archway over the entrance to the State Law Library, the mural, titled *Spirit of the Prairie*, depicts a pioneer mother holding a baby and a second child sitting on the ground at her feet beside their dog. The woman is looking out over the rolling prairie as the wind blows her skirts behind her. The mural was selected as one of twelve best mother-and-child paintings in America in 1931. When quoting a price for the *Spirit of the Prairie* mural at the state capitol building, she wrote to Governor Arthur J. Weaver, "I have made the estimate as low as possible because I wish to feel that I am really making a

Spirit of the Prairie, by Elizabeth Dolan. State Law Library, State Capitol Building, Lincoln, Nebraska. *Author's collection.*

gift to my state." A second, related, painting, *Prairie Woman*, currently adorns the state attorney general's office. It depicts a young pioneer woman looking skyward as she sits on the ground accompanied by a young man. Her dog sits beside her. This painting appears to be a predecessor to *Spirit of the Prairie* and possibly is the same woman when she first arrived on the prairie. It is telling that Dolan portrayed the young woman as looking hopeful. She sees the promise in a future in Nebraska.[244]

During the early 1930s, Dolan painted many murals around Lincoln. These included ten murals for the fiftieth anniversary of the Miller and Paine department store in Lincoln with the theme *Historical Nebraska*. She also painted murals in buildings around the University of Nebraska campus, the Masonic Temple, a Unitarian church and the YWCA and a painting of Hansel and Gretel for the main public library building.[245]

Elizabeth Dolan's success continued into her later life. In 1937, she gave a one-woman show at the Joslyn Memorial Art Gallery in Omaha (chapter 3). She also gave shows around the country and in Paris. In 1936, she reflected:

"On looking back over the years, I feel the same eager enthusiasm to plunge in, inviting beauty to leave even her shadow on walls where she has not passed before." She died in 1948. Her murals still grace the exhibits of Morrill Hall in Lincoln nearly one hundred years later.[246]

Elizabeth Honor Dolan's legacy is a testament to the importance of supportive environments in nurturing creative talents. The foundation laid by the women who directed the University of Nebraska's early art department helped create and preserve an interest in the arts in Nebraska, paving the way for future generations to explore and expand the creative landscape. Their stories highlight the crucial role of women in the development and preservation of the arts. Dolan's work continues to inspire, with her murals serving as enduring symbols of her skill and vision.

9

WRITERS

WILLA CATHER, BESS STREETER ALDRICH AND MARI SANDOZ

Nebraska has produced a remarkable number of literary talents, notable among them three pioneering women writers: Willa Cather, Bess Streeter Aldrich and Mari Sandoz. Each of these authors brought to life the unique experiences and histories of Nebraska through their compelling narratives and vivid character portrayals. Despite their diverse backgrounds and writing styles, Cather, Aldrich and Sandoz have each left an indelible mark on the literary world, ensuring that Nebraska's pioneer history is recognized and celebrated.

Although WILLA CATHER (1873–1947) spent only a brief span of her life in Nebraska, her time in the state had a profound influence on her writing. Cather's family moved from Virginia to Nebraska in the spring of 1883, settling in an area between the Little Blue and Republican Rivers known as the Divide, near the town of Red Cloud. Willa, or Willie as she was known as a child, was only nine years old. The move was hard for her at first. She saw it as an "erasure of personality," but after a little exploration, she came to love her new home. She particularly found comfort in visiting with the immigrant women in the community and listening to stories of their homelands and their experiences settling on the prairie.[247]

After a year of trying to farm on the Divide, Willa's father moved the family into Red Cloud. Cather's mother, Jennie, didn't care for farm life. She was ladylike and couldn't bear the isolation of living out on the prairie. The family also wanted to be closer to a doctor and schools for Willie and her brothers. So, before the winter of 1884 they moved into town, where

Willie's father, Charles, opened a real estate and insurance office. Living in Red Cloud also provided more cultural and social opportunities for young Willie. She spent time with her friends, often putting on theatricals at one another's homes, and attended the local opera house, where many of the shows were musicals. At her friend's home she also met Annie Sadilek, a Bohemian who worked in the household. The Sadilek family lived on a farm near town and experienced a tragedy that would fascinate Cather for the rest of her life. Annie's father, Francis Sadilek, had been a violinist in Prague. When the struggle to support his family as a farmer became too much, he smashed his violin and shot himself. This story of this horrific event served as the basis for several of Cather's stories, including one of her best-known books set in Nebraska, *My Àntonia*.[248]

As a teen, Cather wanted to become a doctor. She learned Latin and Greek and developed her interest in science. She was also inspired by two doctors in Red Cloud: her family's doctor, Dr. G.E. McKeeby, and Robert Damerell. These men often allowed her to accompany them on their house calls. After helping Dr. Damerell by administering chloroform while he amputated a boy's leg, she aspired to become a surgeon.[249]

Unfortunately, the paths to becoming a doctor were not available to Cather. Her family did not have the money to send her to one of the few medical schools in the East, and no local doctor was willing to apprentice her. The best her father could do was send her to the university in Lincoln. Although tuition was free, her father still had to take out a loan to pay the $150 for registration, science lab fees, books, room and board for the nine-month school year. When Cather left for school, she was in a rebellious streak. Always something of a tomboy as a child, during her teenage years she became even more eccentric. She cut her hair short, wore men's clothing and a derby hat, carried a cane and signed her name "William Cather, M.D." When performing in theatricals, she preferred to take on men's roles. This may have been her way of acting out against a society that constricted her options and tried to deny her dream of becoming a doctor. This "rebellion" lasted only until her second year in college, further supporting the idea that she was pushing back against societal norms.[250]

While Cather may have started college wanting to become a doctor, it wasn't long before her interests shifted to more literary aims. Her writing career started when one of her professors sent one of her essays to the *Nebraska State Journal*, who published it. In the essay, Willa wrote about art, literature and the craft of writing. She said, "Art of every kind is an exacting master," and emphasized the hard work and self-discipline required to be an

Portrait of Willa Cather by Carl Van Vechten, 1936. *Library of Congress, Prints & Photographs Division, Carl Van Vechten Collection, LC-USZ62-42538 (b&w film copy neg.).*

artist. She also published her first work of fiction during her first year in college. The short story "Peter" appeared in the Boston magazine *The Mahogany Tree* in May 1892. Inspired by the tragedy of Annie Sadilek's father, the story explored the frustrations of an artist's life, a theme she often turned to in her writing. Willa's literary interests also included founding the campus magazine, *The Lasso*, with her friend Louise Pound (chapter 7) and taking part in the university's Union Literary Society.[251]

Cather helped fund her college career by writing for the *Nebraska State Journal*. Journalism was not something new to her, however. Prior to attending university, she wrote a column for the Red Cloud *Webster County Argus* on high school news. In 1893, she started working for the *Nebraska State Journal* writing drama reviews and columns. Her column, "One Way of Putting It," was unsigned, but the newspaper allowed her to write whatever she wanted. During her college years, she also served as literary editor and later editor of *The Hesperian*, a student publication at the University of Nebraska.[252]

Cather never wanted to become a scholar, unlike her friend Louise Pound. She felt that scholars took the joy out of literature with their overanalysis. Instead, she became a journalist. After graduating from college, she continued working for the *Nebraska State Journal* and took a position as associate editor with *The Courier*, a Lincoln newspaper focused on society, literature and art. The paper was also the official organ of the Nebraska State Federation of Women's Clubs. *The Courier* was not the best fit for Cather. Unlike Nebraska journalist Elia Peattie (chapter 4), Willa had no use for women's clubs. She was determined to have a career and did not want to associate with women who didn't share her ambition to work outside the home. Lack of money cut her journalism career in Lincoln short only a year after graduation. Unable to afford her boardinghouse, Cather had to move home to Red Cloud until she took a job as editor of the *Home Monthly* in Pittsburg. In 1896, she moved to Pennsylvania, and while she visited Nebraska throughout the rest of her life, she never again lived in the state.[253]

Cather's career as a novelist began with the publication of her first novel, *Alexander's Bridge*, in 1912. In the sixteen years between leaving Nebraska and her first novel, she worked as the editor of the *Home Monthly* in Pittsburg and an editor with the *Pittsburgh Leader*, taught high school in Pittsburgh and moved to New York City to work as an editor for *McClure's Magazine*. Cather's first novel set in Nebraska came out in 1913. *O Pioneers!* tells the story of Alexandra Bergson, daughter of Swedish immigrants, as she works to build her farm into one of the best on the Divide. Cather drew on her memories of "old neighbors, once very dear, whom I had almost forgotten in the hurry and excitement of growing up," to incorporate the stories of other immigrant families into the novel. Her early life in Nebraska influenced many of her novels. Memories of the people she knew during her childhood in Nebraska, especially the immigrant women she had found comfort in listening to as a girl, inspired many of her books set in Nebraska. Cather set half of her twelve famous novels in the state: *O Pioneers!* (1913), *The Song of the Lark* (1915), *My Àntonia* (1918), *One of Ours* (1922), *A Lost Lady* (1923) and *Lucy Gayheart* (1935). Cather's novels tell history as it was lived. Unlike Sandoz (discussed later), she was not interested in the facts of what happened but wanted to reflect what the past meant to the people who lived it.[254]

In 1923, her fourth Nebraska novel, *One of Ours*, won the Pulitzer Prize. The book follows six years in the life of a young man of an artistic nature who had grown up on a Nebraska farm. Unhappy with farm life and left adrift after a failed marriage, he enlists in the army and is sent to France. There, he finds contentment in French art and culture, only to be killed in World War I. Literary critics disliked the novel, but the public loved it. Despite the poor reviews, the Pulitzer judges selected the book as the best novel of 1922.[255]

Cather received many other accolades in honor of her literary work. In 1917, the University of Nebraska was the first to award her an honorary doctorate degree. Other honorary degrees followed from the University of Michigan, Columbia University, Yale, University of California–Berkeley, Princeton and Smith College. She was also elected to membership in the National Institute of Arts and Letters in 1929 and later their Academy in 1938. She was posthumously awarded the National Institutes of Arts and Letters Gold Medal.[256]

Willa Cather died in New York in 1947 after suffering a cerebral hemorrhage. Even though she lived in Nebraska for only thirteen years and half of her books are about Nebraska, she is still the most famous author associated with the state. Her six Nebraska novels put the state

Bust of Willa Cather, Nebraska Hall of Fame, State Capitol Building, Lincoln, Nebraska. *Courtesy of Nikolyn McDonald.*

on the literary map and shared the experiences of Nebraskans, especially those who had immigrated from other countries. Her legacy lives on in her books and the work of the National Willa Cather Center in Red Cloud. She was the first woman in the Nebraska Hall of Fame, and since June 2023, her statue has represented Nebraska in the Statuary Hall of the U.S. Capitol building.[257]

ALTHOUGH BESS STREETER ALDRICH (1881–1954) was born and raised in Iowa, she was a Nebraskan in her heart. Her short stories reflect the wholesome and often amusing life of small-town midwestern families and her most famous novels celebrate the tenacity and spirit of the Nebraska pioneer. Aldrich's interest in pioneer stories originated with her parents and grandparents, who were early settlers in northwestern Iowa. Her father came to Iowa from Illinois in 1852, arriving by wagon when there were no railroads west of the Mississippi river. Two years later, Aldrich's maternal widowed grandmother arrived in Iowa with her six children, including Aldrich's eighteen-year-old mother, who had driven a wagon all the way from Illinois. The experiences of her pioneer forebearers served as inspiration for her novels.[258]

Although Bess won prizes for her writing while in her teens, she never planned for it to be her life's work. Instead, she enrolled in the Iowa State Teachers College in Cedar Falls, graduating in 1901. She taught in Boone and Marshalltown, Iowa, and Salt Lake City, before returning to her alma mater, where she served as assistant supervisor in the primary training school. After one year, she quit her job to marry Charles Sweetzer Aldrich, known as "Cap," an attorney and Spanish-American War veteran. Two years later, in 1909, they moved to Elmwood, Nebraska.[259]

Bess's introduction to Nebraska was not the most promising. Cap and John Cobb, Bess's brother-in-law, had bought the bank in Elmwood, Nebraska, a small town about thirty miles outside the capital city, Lincoln. Cap went to Elmwood in advance, leaving Bess, their two-month-old daughter, Bess's mother and sister to follow. The women arrived in the middle of a dust storm. Through the dust, she was searching for their rented cottage when she saw her best upholstered rocking chair on the front porch. An arm of the chair had been broken in shipping. Yet it was all made better by the hot meal and hospitality waiting for them on their arrival at their new home. This small-town welcoming would come to mean a lot to Aldrich. She later recalled how "these characteristics and others of the better features of the small town and its people [are what] I have tried to stress in my short stories and books."[260]

Aldrich started writing in childhood. As a teenager, she sent her first story to a contest held by the *Chicago Record* and won a pocket camera. Later she won five dollars for a story she sent to the *Baltimore News*. She used the money to buy a black chiffon parasol. Prior to her marriage, she had authored articles for teachers' magazines and stories for grade school reading supplements. She also sold her first story, "The Madonna of the Purple Gods," to the *National Home Journal* of St. Louis, Missouri. Writing was only a hobby, though. After moving to Elmwood, it was something she did in between caring for her household and young family. Until 1918, she wrote under the pen name Margaret Dean Stevens out of timidity at having her work read—the writer's version of stage fright.[261]

Although Bess's primary focus was home and family, Cap supported her writing efforts. Aldrich recalled that "he urged me on, pressed me to take more time for writing, encouraged me in every way." To improve her writing skills, she enrolled in a short story correspondence course from the Home Correspondence School of Springfield, Massachusetts. After submitting her first lesson, the instructor wrote back to say that she already had the skills and natural talent to be a successful writer.[262]

In 1911, Aldrich published the first in what would become a regular stream of publications. She sent a story, "The Little House Next Door," to a *Ladies Home Journal* contest. Although she didn't win, they liked her story so much that they bought it for $175. She continued to submit stories to contests, finding that the prizes affirmed her success as a writer. Aldrich's stories were successful because of their wholesomeness and the sense of nostalgia they evoked. Her writing career took off in a period when the world was changing. Urbanization and mechanization were taking over what had once been a country perceived as primarily gentlemen farmers, and the horrors of the first World War shocked the sensitivities of everyone. The "old world" seemed under attack by a brash new world. Aldrich's works, whether her short stories about small-town family life or her pioneer novels, reminded readers of a simpler time that they missed.[263] An article in 1931 said of her work:

> *Bess Streeter Aldrich writes some of the most wholesome and sympathetic fiction on this side of the Atlantic, at a time when most authors are doing flippant, sordid, or sophisticated work....Mrs. Aldrich says, "The trend, of course, has been to write of the fast, high-strung, disintegrating home. That type of home...no more represents America than does my type.... There are not many of us who are writing of small-town financially comfortable, one-man-for-one-woman, clean, decent, and law abiding families....I suppose the idea is that there isn't any drama in that sort of family. But there is birth there, and love, and marriage, and death, and all the ups-and-downs which come to every family in every town, large and small.[264]*

Writing about average family life brought Aldrich her first major success in 1918 with the sale of her first short story in the Mother Mason series. The editor commented that it was one of the finest stories about a mother that he had read. The Mother Mason series was innovative because it did not focus on a single person but on an entire family. D. Appleton and

Company of New York published the Mother Mason stories as Aldrich's first book in 1924.[265]

Aldrich based her Mother Mason stories and her later series about the Cutters on her own family. Bess and Cap had four children who served as a boundless joy as well as inspiration. Mary, the eldest child and only daughter, was close with her mother. They often discussed Bess's writing, and Mary would critique her stories before she sent them to publishers. Jim, her oldest son, was quiet and eventually became an artist. He later provided dust jackets and illustrations for some of his mother's books. Her third child, Chuck, was only twenty months younger than his brother. He was active and worked on farms during the summer. He once saved his money and secretly bought a motorcycle, knowing his mother would not approve. After graduating college, he became an aeronautical engineer. The last Aldrich child, Bob, was seven years younger than Chuck. He shared his mother's writing talent and later became a newspaper writer.[266]

Tragedy struck the Aldrich household when Cap died suddenly in 1925. Bess became a widow and sole supporter of four children ranging from ages four to sixteen. She wrote to a friend, "I'm mighty glad I have my little talent for writing because it's going to be bread and butter for us." As a widow, writing became her primary source of income. She could make more through the sale of one story than she could teaching for a year. After Cap's death, Bess briefly considered leaving their home in Elmwood. In 1922, they had built a large prairie-style home they called The Elms. Ultimately, she stayed there to raise her children in the small-town environment that she cherished.[267]

The year Cap died, Bess published her first novel, *The Rim of the Prairie*. She dedicated the book to her late husband, which was fitting, as he had provided the title. It was a phrase he had often used to describe the rise of land viewed from Bess's study window. All of Aldrich's novels were historical and described pioneer life on the prairie. The book is a love story set in a small town in Nebraska and explores the conflict between country and city, but it is the humble citizens of the fictional town of Maple City that are the most memorable. The book was an ode to the Midwest, the small town she called home on the Nebraska prairie and her husband.[268]

Following the publication of *The Rim of the Prairie*, a local radio program invited Aldrich to speak. At the end of the program, she asked listeners to send anecdotes from their pioneer experiences, as she was interested in that part of Nebraska's history. She expected a trickle of responses but received a flood. The stories she collected along with her mother's

The Elms, home of Bess Streeter Aldrich, Elmwood, Nebraska. *Courtesy of Nikolyn McDonald.*

recollections from her life as a pioneer in Iowa became the inspiration for Aldrich's next book, *A Lantern in Her Hand.* The book was about a pioneer family who came to Nebraska in its early days, suffering both the hardships and triumphs of that period. Abbie Deal, the female lead in the book, is a quiet hero who sacrifices her own ambitions to fulfill the traditional female role of wife, mother and homemaker. Published in 1928, the book became Aldrich's first best-seller.[269]

Aldrich followed *Lantern* in 1931 with a novel about Abbie Deal's granddaughter, titled *A White Bird Flying.* It too became a best-seller and was third in total sales for the year, trailing only behind Pearl S. Buck's *The Good Earth* and fellow Nebraskan Willa Cather's *Shadows on the Rock.* She followed with another success in *Miss Bishop* in 1933. This book was unique in that it tells the full life of a teacher. It follows the character of Ella Bishop through her fifty-year college teaching career, starting in 1876 when she was sixteen and a member of the first class to attend the Midwestern College in Oak River. At the end of her career, bankrupt, forced to resign and feeling resentful about having spent her life helping others rather than looking out for her own future, her former students surprise her with a tribute during her final commencement dinner. As with many of Aldrich's novels, *Miss Bishop* is a composite of teachers she had known throughout her life, possibly including Nebraska English professor Louise Pound (chapter 7).[270]

Miss Bishop was also significant in that it was the only one of Aldrich's books to be made into a motion picture. Bess had been trying to get one of her stories made into a movie since 1917. She traveled to California multiple times during the 1930s trying to stir up interest. In 1935, she even wrote to actress Mary Pickford directly, suggesting that she could play Mother Mason. Pickford offered to read the book and asked when they might meet, but nothing came of it. During Aldrich's 1935 trip, Paramount Pictures hired her to spend two weeks improving the script for the motion picture *Pioneer Woman*. Finally, in 1939, she sold the radio and motion picture rights to *Miss Bishop* to United Artists for $15,000. The movie version was titled *Cheers for Miss Bishop*, with Martha Scott playing the lead and Tay Garnett directing. Aldrich served as a consultant on the movie. *Cheers for Miss Bishop* opened in Lincoln in two separate theaters in January 1941. Aldrich also attended the New York premiere at Radio City Music Hall, where the film ran for thirteen weeks.[271]

Before she retired from writing, Bess Aldrich wrote three other significant books. Published in 1935, *Spring Came on Forever* tells the story of three generations of Nebraskans between the 1860s and 1930s. She spent the next three years working on *Song of Years*, published in 1939. Loosely based on the story of her grandfather, Zimri Streeter, it tells the story of the settlement of northeastern Iowa. The book initially ran as a serial in the *Saturday Evening Post*. It was an immediate best-seller when it came out. Finally, she published her last novel, *The Lieutenant's Lady*, in 1942. Based on the diaries of a young woman and her soldier husband, it tells the story of how the young woman traveled up the Missouri River to meet the man she would marry at a remote fort in the Dakotas in the 1860s. Like her earlier works, Aldrich spent nearly a year on research to make sure she made the story as authentic as possible. While not as big a seller as some of her earlier works, it still made the best-seller list for twenty-two weeks.[272]

Bess Streeter Aldrich was a generous woman, both with her time and her money. Among her various church and civic activities, she was involved in founding the Elmwood Women's Club, the first library in Elmwood, and was a charter member of the Nebraska Writers Guild, serving as its president in 1928.[273] Her most generous act, however, she refused to have known during her lifetime. During the Great Depression, the American Exchange

Bank of Elmwood, the bank her husband and brother-in-law had started and of which she was one of three stockholders, faced closure because of Roosevelt's 1933 bank holiday. Aldrich wouldn't let that happen. Although she was busy writing *Miss Bishop*, she took time to visit the state banking department chief. She told him:

> *You do not know the amount of income and savings I have had; I suspect they are larger than you suppose. But if it takes all, to the last cent I have, I shall not permit that bank to close. If you will state the amount of cash necessary to keep the bank open at this time, I will have it ready for you within a few days. If more shall be required later, I will furnish it.*[274]

After that visit, she cashed in enough securities and jewelry to cover the deficit, and the bank stayed open. She insisted that her act remain secret until after her death.[275]

Aldrich received many honors both during her life and posthumously. She received a medal for distinguished service to her state by the Lincoln Kiwanis Club and an honorary doctorate of letters degree from the University of Nebraska in 1934, and in 1971, she was the second woman inducted into the Nebraska Hall of Fame, after Nebraska's other famous woman author Willa Cather.[276]

By 1943, after the publication of *The Lieutenant's Lady* and *Miss Bishop* being made into a movie, Aldrich was financially secure enough that she no longer had to write to support herself. A few years later, she moved to Lincoln to be closer to her daughter. After her move to Lincoln, she wrote less, with only about one short story published a year. Her fourteenth and final book, a collection of short stories titled *The Bess Streeter Aldrich Reader*, came out in 1950. Bess Streeter

Bust of Bess Streeter Aldrich, Nebraska Hall of Fame, State Capitol Building, Lincoln, Nebraska. *Courtesy of Nikolyn McDonald.*

Aldrich died from cancer in 1954 at the age of seventy-three. Shortly before lapsing into a coma before her death, she told her daughter Mary, "I have written my books. I have raised my family. However this turns out will be all right." She was buried next to Cap in the Elmwood Cemetery.[277]

UNLIKE CATHER AND ALDRICH, novelist and historian MARI SANDOZ (1896–1966) was born and raised in Nebraska. She spent her early life in the Sandhills, a region of the state that contributed to early descriptions of the Great Plains as the Great American Desert. The Sandhills are not a desert, however, but an area of grassy, rolling hills dotted with lakes that are excellent for cattle ranching. Sandoz expressed her love for the region and its history in her writings, often focusing on the relationship between humans and the land.

Sandoz was the oldest child of Swiss immigrant Jules Sandoz and his fourth wife, Mary Fehr. Jules was a homesteader in the Niobrara River region of northwestern Nebraska when Mary, called Mari (pronounced Mahr-ee) to distinguish her from her mother, was born. Mari had a challenging childhood. Her father had an unpredictable temper and nearly beat her to death when she was an infant. Her family was impoverished and had an extremely low social standing in whatever community they lived in, largely because of her father's belligerent reputation. As the oldest child in the family, she was often responsible for caring for her younger siblings and taking care of chores around the house while her mother farmed. Her father was also very restrictive and forbade her from leaving the family's farm. Mari's only social interactions for many years were with the Native American children who came with their parents to visit Jules, whom they considered a friend. The only reason she started school at age nine was because someone in the county reported that the Sandoz children were truant and an official came out to the farm. Her first year of school lasted only six weeks.[278]

Mari's aptitude for learning quickly became clear, however. Even though she was already nine years old and only spoke Swiss-German, within three months of schooling she caught up with her classmates. Once she learned to read, she was a voracious reader and worked to learn English well enough to write her own stories. When she was eleven, the *Omaha Daily News* published her first story on their junior page. She wrote the story in secret because her parents thought writing was a waste of time. When she shared her success with them, her father was so furious he locked her in the cellar.[279]

Mari's family situation improved when she was fourteen. Her father's primary occupation was helping locate settlers, and with the Kincaid Act opening the Sandhills to settlement, it was a promising situation. So he moved the family to a homestead in the Sandhills. Since Mari's mother had just had a baby, he sent Mari and her younger brother to hold the claim. It was her first taste of true freedom. Other opportunities followed. The family's social standing improved in their new community, and Jules even let Mari attend a barn dance when she was fifteen.[280]

Sandoz finished eighth grade at the county school. As far as her parents were concerned, that was all the education she needed. Although she had only four and a half years of schooling, she took and passed the rural teaching exam and began teaching country school. She taught school in Sheridan and Cheyenne Counties on and off between 1913 and 1920. She also worked for a time in Osceola as a stenographer. In 1914, she married a local rancher, Wray Macumber, but the union lasted only five years. Afterward, Sandoz never spoke about those years. It was a part of her life she wanted to put behind her. After her divorce, Mari went to live with cousins on the Niobrara rather than stay with her parents. She didn't stay there very long, however. In the fall of 1919, she and her cousin Rosalie moved to Lincoln to attend the Lincoln Business College.[281]

Mari knew from childhood that she wanted to be a writer. After attending business school in Lincoln and working a few years back west, she set her sights on a college degree. In the summer of 1922, she returned to Lincoln to enroll in the University of Nebraska. Although she didn't have the high school credits required to qualify for college, she wore down the dean of the Teachers College until he allowed her to enroll. Financing her degree was another challenge. Throughout her college career, she held down various jobs, including teaching, working for a drug laboratory, proofreading newspapers, conducting research for the Nebraska State Historical Society, grading for professors and serving as editor of the *School Executive Magazine*. Her tenacity served her well, and her professors acknowledged her talent. During her second year, one of her professors sent her short essay "Prairie Fire" to the English department's publication *Freshman Scrapbook*. The recognition solidified her determination to continue writing.[282]

Sandoz also found support from English professor Louise Pound (chapter 7). Pound, whose interests were in American English and folklore, encouraged Sandoz to write in her own Sandhills idiom, rather than conforming to standard English. Pound also supported Mari's writing and invited her to gatherings, where she was often read her work. Sandoz may even have tried to emulate Pound's particular aesthetic, taking her fashion cues from the professor in dying her hair red to match Pound's red-gold braids and later dressing in similar tweeds.

Mari Sandoz, half-length portrait, facing slightly right, *World Telegram* photo by Al Aumuller, 1938. *Library of Congress, Prints & Photographs Division*, New York World-Telegram *and the* Sun *Newspaper Photograph Collection, LC-USZ62-117537 DLC (b&w film copy neg.).*

Mari continued to find success with short story publications during college. In 1926, she won honorable mention in *Harper's* intercollegiate contest for the short story "Fearbitten." Her story "The Vine," about two homesteaders and their relationship to the land, appeared in the first issue of the university's publication, *Prairie Schooner*, in 1927. These were all collegiate publications, however. Getting published in a major publication was more challenging. She sent stories to magazines such as *Harper's*, the *Saturday Evening Post* and *Cosmopolitan*, but they were always rejected. Sandoz had plenty of short stories, essays and even the beginnings of a novel, but no publishers seemed interested.[283]

In 1928, the *Prairie Schooner* published a second of her short stories, "Old Potato Face," notable for its use of the idiom of western Nebraska. Not long after, Mari obtained a literary agent. Through connections made in her recent membership in Quill, a woman's writing group that started up in Lincoln during the 1920s, she contacted the New York agent Margaret Christie. Christie worked to get Mari's work in front of editors but found no more success than Mari had on her own. She was able to explain why success was so elusive:

> It seems that at the moment they are not particularly interested in good writing and they are definitely uninterested in unhappy, stark realistic characteristic stories....The consensus of demand is for a fast moving, hold-the-interest, romantic-angled up-to-the-minute tale. They also want comedy, light in structure, well plotted and sophisticated.[284]

This, of course, was not what Sandoz wrote. Sandoz wrote about what she knew. Her stories were usually gloomy and realistic.

During the fall of 1928, Mari's father died. Although their relationship had been contentious and Jules had never supported her desire to write, Mari was with him at the end, and his last words to her were, "Why don't you write my life some time?" It was all she needed. Christie had encouraged her to write longer works, and Mari had in mind to write her father's story for quite some time. She had even been collecting information on his life, but it was his blessing that allowed her to move forward with the project. The decision to write about her father would eventually put Sandoz on the path to success.[285] It was not an easy path, however. Returning to her parents' farm in the fall of 1929 to continue her research, she found that her mother had destroyed most of Jules's papers and she refused to help. Mari salvaged what she could from the damp meat house where her mother had tossed the papers and started to piece her father's life together. Sandoz also parted ways with her agent, Margaret Christie. She had become disillusioned with Christie's inability to place her work. The relationship had produced one important sale to the *North American Review*, a two-part article titled "The Kinkaider Comes and Goes." The article was significant in that it proved that publishers and readers were interested in the Sandhills.[286]

In the early 1930s, Sandoz struggled financially. She was writing, but her work wasn't selling. She found part-time work as a proofreader for the *Lincoln Journal and Star*, but it wasn't enough to live on. In the fall of 1931, however, she was hired at the Nebraska State Historical Society. She continued to work on *Old Jules*, finishing it and sending it out twice in 1932 with no success. In October 1932, she sent the manuscript to the *Atlantic's* nonfiction contest. Although they held it for eight months, considering it as one of five finalists, they ultimately rejected it. By the fall of 1933, Mari was ready to give up. She planned to return to the Sandhills and gathered a few friends for a ceremonial burning of her work in a galvanized tub behind her apartment building in Lincoln. It is unclear what exactly she burned, since copies of most of her work still existed later in her life, but she liked to feed the myth that she had burned almost everything.[287]

Mari returned to the Sandhills but found she couldn't give up writing. She set up a writing studio in an old garage on her family's ranch and returned to work on her book *Slogum House*, a novel she had been working on when she started her father's biography. In August 1934, Mari finally found someone willing to publish *Old Jules*. Caxton Press in Idaho was interested but wanted her to split the cost since they were a small company. Having no money to contribute, Mari declined, but they offered to publish the book if their financial situation changed. In the meantime, she contacted *Atlantic* about entering *Old Jules* in their nonfiction contest again. She had completely rewritten the book and changed the fictional names in the work for real ones. The *Atlantic* agreed, so she sent it yet again for the 1935 contest. This time she won.[288]

By 1935, Mari was back in Lincoln working for the Nebraska State Historical Society, supervising federally funded projects and editing *Nebraska History Magazine*. The publication of *Old Jules* was a life-changing event. She quit her job to write full time that September. The book was a critical success. It was named Book-of-the-Month club selection for November 1935 and led to her representation by two literary agents. Even the film industry was interested in the story, with MGM taking an option for $2,500. The book was shocking, however, in both its domestic scenes and its unromantic depiction of the West. Mari did not pull any punches in her depiction of her father's brutality and vulgarity. The book received mixed reception in Nebraska. Many of Mari's friends were surprised, not having known she had been working on a longer piece, especially one that was largely nonfiction. The Nebraska State Historical Society honored the Sandoz family at their annual meeting in the fall of 1935, with Mari giving the dinner address. Some state residents were less laudatory, questioning how she portrayed the Sandhills and complaining about her frank portrayal of her father.[289]

Mari's next two books were the novels *Slogum House* (1937) and *Capital City* (1939). Generally, her novels were more controversial and less successful than her historical works. Her early novels, such as *The Tom Walker* (1947), were allegories intended to call out pre- and post-war concerns such as the rise of fascism and the Red Scare. Her later novels, *Miss Morissa* (1955) and *Son of the Gamblin' Man* (1960), based on historical people or composites of historical people, included so much historical detail that the characters were largely lost. Citizens of Lincoln, Nebraska's capital, especially disliked *Capital City* because they thought it was about them, despite Sandoz's assurance that it was a composite of ten midwestern cities.[290] As one review in the *Omaha Morning World-Herald* said, "Mari Sandoz is a violent hater. She hates greed. So she wrote a novel about greed personified by Gulla Slogum, and 'Slogum House' made a lot of people mad. Now 'Capital City' will make a lot more people more mad." Another reviewer, however, applauded Sandoz, referring to the author and her books as "fearless." The situation in Lincoln, however, may have become too much for Mari. [291] She abruptly moved to Denver in 1940. Although she claimed it was to be closer to research materials on the book she was starting about Oglala Lakota Chief Crazy Horse, some of her friends suspected otherwise.

Sandoz's best works were her histories. Like *Old Jules*, these works were historical fact turned into a narrative format. Mari was relentless in her historical research, searching the historical record and visiting the places and talking to people who had experienced the events she wrote about. Her histories, of course, focused on western topics and locations near to her heart. *Crazy Horse* (1942) and *Cheyenne Autumn* (1953) are considered two of her best works. Both are based on history that occurred in the Nebraska panhandle's Pine Ridge area. *Crazy Horse* was unique in that it tells the story of the Oglala and their defeat of Custer at the Little Bighorn from the Lakota perspective. Sandoz saw Crazy Horse as a hero and considered the book her finest work. Years after the book's publication, she wrote to her friend Mamie Meredith, saying:

> *I've always felt that the underlying theme of Crazy Horse, the destiny fore-ordained for him and the people he led, no matter how great his personal virtue, is Greek in its tragic implications. I've always felt, ever since my introduction to Greek literature, that the Plains Indians had close affinity for the Greeks in their sense of honor and honor lost.*[292]

Although Sandoz was proud of the work, it was not a best-seller and received mixed reviews. Preconceived notions about American Indians influenced some critics, and they didn't believe Mari's portrayal. Others took issue with the book for the same reason some had taken issue with *Old Jules*: it was neither purely history nor purely fiction. Western writers, such as Wallace Stegner and John G. Neihardt, however, praised the work, along with Native Americans who revered Crazy Horse. One Oglala even said that Sandoz wrote "'just like the good old Lakotas spoke." Publication of *Crazy Horse* established Mari's reputation as a historian and a writer.[293]

Cheyenne Autumn was the third of her pseudo-biographies. It tells the story of two Cheyenne chiefs, Dull Knife and Little Wolf, who led their bands from a reservation in Oklahoma Territory to their homeland in the northern Great Plains. Captured by the military, they broke out of the barracks at Fort Robinson in the Nebraska panhandle. Most of the Cheyenne who escaped were hunted down and killed. Sandoz portrayed it as an epic tragedy, highlighting the destruction of the Cheyenne people's way of life. *Cheyenne Autumn* received more critical acclaim than *Crazy Horse*, and it appealed to readers more as well. The Northern Cheyenne were so pleased with the book that one of the council members asked Sandoz to write a sequel

Bust of Mari Sandoz, Nebraska Hall of Fame, State Capitol Building, Lincoln, Nebraska. *Courtesy of Nikolyn McDonald.*

chronicling the tribe's history up to their settlement on the Tongue River Reservation in Montana.[294]

Sandoz followed up these two works with her Great Plains Series, *The Buffalo Hunters* (1954), *The Cattlemen* (1958) and *The Beaver Men* (1964), which tell the history of western settlement using animals as the focal point. Her other significant nonfiction works from later in her career include *These Were the Sioux* (1961), *Love Song to the Plains* (1961) and *The Battle of the Little Bighorn* (1966).[295]

Sandoz received several honors during her lifetime. The University of Nebraska–Lincoln gave her an honorary doctorate of literature degree in 1950. She was also the first person to receive an award for distinguished service from the Native Sons and Daughters of Nebraska. Posthumously, she was inducted into the Nebraska Hall of Fame in 1976.[296]

Sandoz moved to New York City in 1943, but she never liked it. She moved to be closer to eastern publishers and archival repositories, which held the historical information she needed for her research. She thought it would be temporary and was always homesick for the Plains. In her New York apartment, she put up reminders of the West on her walls: an old cowboy hat, a combination bullet mold and reloading tool her father had used for repairs and a map she had been working on of the movements of the Plains Indians before the reservation period. She never returned to the West. In 1954, she was diagnosed with breast cancer. Ever the workaholic, she worked right up to surgery and was dictating a story the day after. The breast cancer returned in 1963, but again it barely slowed her down. In the fall of 1964, however, the cancer returned yet again, this time in her bones. Up to the last few months of her life, Mari Sandoz continued to write, finishing her book on the Battle of the Little Bighorn. She died in New York City in 1966 and was buried on her family's ranch in the Sandhills. The historical marker later placed at her birthplace in Sheridan County notes, "Her own aim was to understand all of life by understanding this one part of it: how man shaped the Plains country, and how it shaped him."[297]

The lives and works of Mari Sandoz, Bess Streeter Aldrich and Willa Cather have left an indelible mark on the literary landscape, particularly in their depictions of Nebraska and pioneer life. Each author brought unique perspectives and narrative styles that not only reflected their firsthand experiences but also provided rich, historical insights into the lives of Nebraskans. Their collective contributions underscore the importance of storytelling in preserving cultural heritage and influencing future generations. As we continue to explore and appreciate their literary legacies, we gain a deeper understanding of the historical and social contexts that shaped their writing, ensuring that their voices remain a vibrant part of our cultural consciousness.

10

ENTREPRENEURS

ESSIE DAVIS AND ROSE BLUMKIN

Nebraska has been home to many women who have contributed to its economic successes. Among these, two stand out for their extraordinary enterprising spirit and business acumen: Essie Davis and Rose Blumkin. Both women overcame obstacles to build thriving businesses from the ground up, proving their resilience, innovation and an unyielding drive for success. Essie Buchanan Davis, known as the "Lady of the Sandhills," was a formidable figure in the world of ranching. Managing the vast OLO Ranch, she overcame significant challenges, including severe debt and natural disasters to build a prosperous enterprise. Rose Blumkin, affectionately known as Mrs. B, founded the Nebraska Furniture Mart and built it into the largest furniture store in America. Her journey from a small Russian village to becoming a leading Nebraska businesswoman is a testament to her determination and innovative merchandising strategies. Both women embodied the pioneer spirit, representing homesteaders seeking land and opportunity and the many immigrants who came to Nebraska in search of a better life.

ESSIE BUCHANAN DAVIS (1882–1966) came from humble beginnings. Born in Indianola, Illinois, she was the oldest child in a poor family. Her father made his living by importing horses, which eventually brought the family to Ogallala, Nebraska, the cowboy capital of the state. There, her father found success trading Belgian stallions. Essie worked in a millinery store in Ogallala, but she also attended the occasional stock show with her father. At the age of thirty-one, likely considered an old maid, she met A. Thane Davis at a stock show in Denver. Davis, who went by A.T., was a Cherry County, Nebraska, rancher in his mid-fifties. After a short engagement, the couple married and took a honeymoon to Ketchikan, Alaska, before returning to Davis's ranch. Essie, who had never lived on a ranch before, knew nothing about what she was getting into.[298]

The Davis family originally homesteaded in Red Willow County, Nebraska, but A.T.'s father died when he was only fifteen. In 1888, A.T. and his mother decided that ranching would be more successful than farming and moved to Cherry County, about sixteen miles from the town of Hyannis. They were one of the first families to settle in what became known as Davis Valley and built a two-thousand-acre ranch.[299] By the time Essie came to live at A.T.'s OLO Ranch, it was a three-thousand-acre spread with $80,000 in debt. A new barn was nearing completion, and the main house was still being built. For the meantime, the newlyweds lived in a one-room building with curtains for room dividers. A.T. was so unused to being married and distracted by thoughts of returning to his ranch that he accidentally left his new wife at the train station upon their arrival home. He realized his mistake only when he got close to the ranch and remembered that he had to carry her over the threshold. He returned to town to find that the ever-resourceful Essie had taken a room at the hotel. Fortunately for A.T., Essie could be forgiving.[300]

A.T. and Essie had a happy marriage for eighteen months. They welcomed a son, Thane, and the ranch continued to prosper. But Essie suddenly found herself a widow when A.T. died in Omaha after a brief illness. A.T. left her with a four-month-old son, a 3,500-acre ranch and $80,000 in debt. Essie's sister, Floy, came to help her, but many tried to convince Essie to sell out and move on. Ranching in the 1910s was demanding work, hard enough for a man they said, let alone a woman. Essie would not give up everything her husband had worked for. "I knew almost nothing of ranching," she later told a reporter. "But I thought I'd rather try it than be a quitter." She stuck it out, hired a foreman to help and sought the answers she needed from experts, noting, "There was never a time when I asked for help that I didn't figure out who knew the answer, and I followed advice to the letter."[301]

Essie had a lot to learn about the ranching business. She was an apt student and learned about cattle and how to keep them, how to improve the range, deal with cattle dealers, balance income versus expenses and manage the men she hired to work on the ranch. The 1904 Kinkaid Act, which opened the Sandhills to homesteading, made it challenging to support a herd because homesteaders had taken up so much of the land. That was the source of the

Sandhills cattle.
Courtesy of Cilinda Meyer-Scheideler.

debt she inherited from her husband. He has spent $80,000 largely buying up additional grazing land from settlers who failed in homesteading.[302]

Essie was determined to preserve her husband's legacy, and with the help of her sister Floy, serving as secretary and companion, her brother E.C. Buchanan and later her son, Thane, she succeeded. She increased the size of the ranch nearly tenfold to thirty thousand acres and had 2,500 Hereford cattle. Not only did she grow the ranch, but she paid it off as well, including the $80,000 debt she inherited from her husband. She sent her son, Thane, to the University of Nebraska College of Agriculture, and he eventually became her partner on the ranch. She also built up the ranch stead, creating her own small town. There were two modern large brick houses, a swimming pool and various outbuildings. She also installed a water system, hard surfaced roads and runways for the planes the family eventually came to own. The *Lincoln Journal Star* noted in 1941, "Her ranch house resembles a resort hotel—modern in every respect."[303]

Essie also developed her knowledge of cattle, becoming an expert on Herefords. She decided that the best way to improve the ranch's chances was to improve the herd from common range stock to a thoroughbred line. Drawing on her early life attending stock shows with her father, she attended sales and shows and watched how the men selected the best breeding stock. Soon she was buying the best of the stock out from under the men. She personally managed the yearly sale of her cattle for many years. The *Nebraska State Journal* noted, "Her favorite hobby is developing purebred bull calves.

Each year she selects a dozen of her best ones from her herd, allowing no one else the privilege of choosing them."[304]

Success didn't come without struggle, however. Weather was a constant concern in the Sandhills and could decimate cattle herds. Essie once bought four hundred head of cattle from Mexico and lost them the day after their arrival to a blizzard. Cattle from Texas and Mexico were unused to the climate and could quickly perish in a blizzard, as ice would cover their faces and bodies, taking their breath away or simply freezing them to death. To combat blizzards, Essie and Thane planted trees as "outdoor barns" to provide better shelter for their herds. Cattle weren't the only ones at risk from blizzards. They could often come up fast with no warning no matter how nice the day started. During one such occasion, Essie, Floy

Sandhills cow and calf. *Courtesy of Cilinda Meyer-Scheideler.*

and Thane found themselves caught away from home when a blizzard blew in. Their car stalled in a deep sand blowout, for the roads in the Sandhills were also notoriously bad, and they had to walk a mile through knee-deep snow until they found the safety of an abandoned sod house. Essie and Floy were particularly at a disadvantage because they were in dresses and silk hose. They had not expected snow when they started out. Essie recalled:

> *Our limbs were frozen. We had to render our own first aid. In the morning the cowboys came out to feed cattle and rescued us....It took a team of four horses to pull the sled on which we rode, and a half-day was spent in going the three miles to our home.*[305]

The first fear for ranchers might be blizzards, but the second was grass fires. Essie recalled one spring grass fire nearly cost her their home. A neighbor accidentally started a grass fire when burning off an unused pasture in high wind and it quickly spread to the OLO. The fire grew to forty-five to fifty miles long and fifteen miles wide. People came from as far as one hundred miles away to help fight it. The women at the OLO gave all their time to telephoning and answering calls while they waited for news. Once the fire was contained, Essie found herself with a host of hungry firefighters, and she wasn't going to let them down. She cleared out her stores to feed the men who had saved her home, as the fire had come within a few miles of her house. "I began frying eggs, two large skillets full at a time, and kept this up from 6:30 to 10:30 p.m.," she said. This on top of providing two cases of pork and beans, bread and crackers and "cases and cases of coffee." Hospitality was a small price to pay compared to what might have been. The Davises ended up losing some calves and 80 percent of the OLO's grassland and feed in that fire.[306]

Besides being one of the biggest ranch owners in the Sandhills during the first half of the twentieth century, Essie Davis also holds the distinction of being the first woman president of a credit association in the United States. A group of cattlemen sought her out to head their cooperative bank, the Alliance, Nebraska Production Credit Association, in the late 1930s. The production credit association, or PCA, formed in response to falling cattle prices and failing banks during the Great Depression. The federal government authorized the creation of PCAs to help ranchers and farmers get goods to market during this period of economic hardship. Within four years, the association had loaned $3.5

million to ranchers in western Nebraska. Essie remained president of the Alliance PCA for ten years.[307]

Essie was also active in politics. A staunch Democrat, she served on the Nebraska State Democratic Central Committee as vice-chairwoman in 1944. Although Governor Val Peterson was a Republican, he admired Essie enough to appoint her to the Highway Advisory Committee. He also asked her to serve as a founder of the Investors of Nebraska Insurance company. Peterson complained to the board, "You don't have enough Democrats and you don't have any women," and then he suggested to include Essie. Although encouraged to run for national office herself, Essie didn't want to leave her beloved Sandhills. She received many invitations to visit politicians around the country, including inauguration receptions at the White House and to dine with Eleanor Roosevelt. She attended Democratic conventions, where she met Adlai Stevenson and John F. Kennedy, and even received a Christmas card from the Kennedys.[308]

Unsurprisingly, Essie was independent and not afraid of sharing her opinion. She claimed that she was "ornery as hell!," but that it was more persistence than stubbornness. She did, however, have a habit of getting her own way. Essie considered remarrying once, to former Colorado governor George Carlson, but she had become too independent and didn't want a man to take over her life and business. An earlier attempt at taking on a partner had not gone very well when her partner refused to take orders or advice from a woman, even though she had 2,500 head of cattle to his 300.[309]

Essie might have been independent and opinionated, but she also believed in the value of kindness. She once said, "A woman's ranch problems are no different than a man's, except that they are often emphasized or exaggerated." Acknowledging that one of the most challenging and life-changing decisions she ever made was to continue with the ranch after A.T.'s death, she recalled:

I decided right then to deal as a man would. No crybaby stuff was ever to enter in. I would take my losses as a matter of course, or maybe, ignorance. Best of all, as I have found out over the years, I decided to live my life each day and live it so that I could look any man in the face and tell him to go to hell![310]

But she believed in being humble and learning from those more knowledgeable around her and not being afraid of challenging work.

To say that it has been easy would be gross understatement, nor would one wish it otherwise, for it is only after a long hard battle has been fought that we can appreciate what is well worthwhile in accomplishment. The hard times brought the sure reward of having some kind cattleman ready to help me and give me a boost over the top.[311]

Above all, she believed in having faith in yourself, and she certainly played that out in her life.

Besides her success in ranching and work in politics, Essie won widespread recognition as an agricultural leader and conservationist. In 1939, she was the first woman to win the Master Farmer Award, which she received for efficiency in ranching. She also received the Nebraska Builder Award from the University of Nebraska in 1963. It was the highest non-academic service award the university awards.[312] Essie died at the age of eighty-three in Scottsdale, Arizona. She is buried in Hyannis, Nebraska, near her beloved ranch.

Born in Russia, Rose Blumkin (1893–1998) overcame many hardships, including language barriers and economic challenges, to establish a successful business based on the principles of honesty and low prices. Her innovative merchandising strategies and determination allowed her to overcome obstacles and expand her store. Her story exemplifies the immigrant experience in the United States and the pursuit of the American Dream.

Rose Gorelick was one of eight children growing up in a two-room log home in the small village of Shidreen, near Minsk. Her father was a rabbi, and her mother ran a grocery store. Rose never went to school, but she learned to calculate figures in her head while helping her mother in her store. She once said, "I'm born, thank God, with brains. In Russia you don't have no adding machine or nothing, so you have to use your head. So I always used it."[313]

At thirteen, she set out with a new pair of shoes to find a job in the city. She didn't want to wear out her new shoes too quickly, however, so she carried them the eighteen miles to the train. Once in town, she went to twenty-five stores seeking employment, but each one told her she was too young. Rose was not one to give up. During her job search, she heard about a shop girl who left for America, so she woke up early the next morning and went to the shop. Before anyone else showed up she had readied the store and started making sales. Providing a glimpse into the woman she would become, she wasn't going to wait for someone to offer her something, she just took it. By the time she was sixteen, she was managing the store and its six male employees.[314]

In 1914, Rose married Isadore Blumkin, a shoe salesperson. The couple planned to immigrate to America, but their plans changed when World War I broke out and Isadore had to flee Russia to escape conscription into the czar's army. They didn't have enough money to both go, so Rose stayed behind. Three years later she joined him after an arduous journey of her own that involved a trip on the Trans-Siberian Railroad to the Chinese border, where she had to bluff her way past a Russian border guard. She told him that she was on a trip to buy leather for the army and promised him a bottle of vodka when she returned. After that she made her way to Japan and bought a first-class ticket to the United States, but it turned out to be a six-week journey on a peanut boat to Seattle. When she finally arrived in the United States, she had no entry permit. Fortunately, she was allowed into the country, and an immigrant society sent her west to join her husband in Fort Dodge, Iowa.[315]

The couple spent two years in Fort Dodge before moving to Nebraska. Omaha had a large group of Russian immigrants, and Rose, who only learned English once her children were old enough to teach her, wanted to be around people she could talk to. Isidore opened a secondhand clothing store, and Rose helped him with the store through the Great Depression, while she also raised their four children: son Louie and daughters Frances, Sylvia and Cynthia. In 1922, she helped her parents, a brother, four sisters and a cousin immigrate to America, enlarging their family circle.[316]

Rose had a knack for business. Once during the early years of the Depression, she had ten thousand circulars printed up that offered to dress a man "from head to toe for $5." It included a suit, hat, shoes, socks, shirt, tie and underwear. Her husband's store took in $800 the next day. In 1937, Rose decided to open her own business. She borrowed $500 from her brother and opened a furniture store across the alley from her husband's clothing store. Her business plan was to undersell other furniture stores by charging customers only 10 percent over cost.[317]

Her first challenge was getting merchandise to sell. Suppliers didn't want to give her credit, and name-brand manufacturers didn't appreciate her selling items below list price. So Rose traveled to Kansas City and Chicago by train to buy merchandise at 5 percent above wholesale, and then shipped it to Omaha, where she marked it up 10 percent and still sold at a lower price than other retailers in the city. "I became a good bootlegger, the best in town," she later said. "The more they boycotted me, the harder I worked." Once, desperate for money to pay her suppliers, she sold the furniture from her own home to make ends meet. Her daughter Frances recalled, "We all cried….There were no beds, no table. We sat on orange crates, slept on mattresses on the floor." But Rose reassured her children, "Someday, I'll give you everything. Now we have to pay our bills." Short of cash in 1950, Rose rented the old City Auditorium in Omaha and turned it into a giant furniture showroom. Over three days, she sold $250,000 in furniture, allowing her to pay her debts, including a $50,000 bank loan she had taken out to stay afloat.[318]

Rose's Nebraska Furniture Mart, which had started in a basement in 1937, moved into a building one block long by 1945. In 1970, they expanded even further into a building in West Omaha that was three blocks long with 300,000 square feet of display, 500,000 square feet of warehouse and 25 acres of parking. The downtown location closed in 1980. As the store grew, Rose, known to her customers as Mrs. B, regularly zipped around her large store on her motorized scooter. Her credo was "sell cheap and tell the truth." She worked sixty-hour weeks and never took vacations. She was unstoppable. When a tornado tore the roof off the West Omaha store in 1975, she kept going. When the store suffered a fire, she opened back up the next day and gave the firemen a free television for their efforts in saving her business. Even after walking out after a dispute with her grandsons, she opened Mrs. B's Warehouse next door. She was ninety-five years old. They reconciled a few years later, and she sold the business to the Furniture Mart but continued to work there selling carpet. In 1993, she spent her one hundredth birthday selling carpet in her store, one of her favorite things to do.[319]

Some of the highest praise Mrs. B received was from Nebraska businessman Warren Buffett, one of the most successful investors in the world. He praised her business acumen on multiple occasions, noting that you could "put her up against the top graduates of the top business schools or chief executives of the Fortune 500….She'd run rings around them." He also said, "They'll be studying her in business history books for decades to come." In 1983, Rose sold the Furniture Mart to Buffett's Berkshire Hathaway for $55 million. Wanting to ensure that the business's future would be settled after her death, Buffett accepted the business without even an inventory. As Mrs. B told the story, Buffett walked in one day and asked her if she wanted to sell her store to him. When she said yes, he asked how much she wanted. She told him $60 million, and he went back to the office and returned with a check. She told him, "You are crazy. Where are your lawyers? Where are your accountants?"

The Rose Blumkin Theater, 2001 Farnam Street, Omaha, Nebraska. *Courtesy of Nikolyn McDonald.*

All he replied was "I trust you more." For his part, Buffett said "We gave Mrs. B a check for $55 million, and she gave us her word. That made for an even exchange." Berkshire Hathaway ended up with a 90 percent interest in the business while Rose's son, Louie Blumkin, and his family kept a minority share and continued to manage the store.[320]

While Rose had few interests outside her business and her family, she had many philanthropic pursuits around Omaha. She gave $1 million to build a nursing home next to the Jewish Community Center. When the Astro Theater was to be torn down in 1981, she bought it. The building held special memories for her as the location where her daughter Frances had won a singing contest. She renovated the theater, and it reopened as the Rose Blumkin Performing Arts Center, or the Rose, as it is more commonly called.[321]

Mrs. B received many honorary degrees, including an honorary doctoral degree in commercial science from New York University in 1984, when she was ninety years old. The honor recognized "world-class captains of business and industry" and she was the first woman to receive it. She also received an honorary doctor of law degree from Creighton University. She is recognized as Omaha's greatest businesswoman; received the Distinguished Nebraskan Award from the Nebraska Society of Washington, D.C.; and was inducted into the Nebraska Business Hall of Fame in 1993.[322]

In 1984, a newspaper reporter asked what advice Mrs. B had to impart. She said:

> First, honesty. Second, hard work. Next, if you don't get the job you want right away, tell them you'll take anything. If you're good, they'll keep you.... You struggle, you work hard, you hope, sometimes your wishes come true, sometimes not....My wish came true. I used to say, "I'm not going to stay in the basement forever. Someday I'm gonna have a good-looking store."[323]

Mrs. B never officially retired. She continued to sell carpet up until the last year of her life, although her workdays became shorter and her absences more frequent as her health declined. In 1998, she died from old age at 104 with her daughters at her side. Her grandson Robert Batt noted that the family kept the Furniture Mart open during her memorial service: "I don't think she would want us to close." Such was her devotion and love for the business she had built.[324]

The entrepreneurial journeys of Essie Buchanan Davis and Rose Blumkin are profound testaments to the resilience and innovative spirit of women in

Nebraska's history. Both women, despite starting from humble beginnings, rose to prominence through sheer determination and ingenuity. Essie Buchanan Davis transformed a heavily indebted ranch into a flourishing enterprise, overcoming personal and environmental hardships. Rose Blumkin emigrated from Russia and built one of the largest businesses in the state, embodying the quintessential American Dream. Their legacies are marked by not only their business successes but also by their contributions to their communities and the pioneering spirit they represent. These stories serve as enduring inspirations, illustrating that with perseverance and vision, remarkable achievements are possible.

NOTES

1. Homesteaders: Elizabeth Scott and Alice Fish

1. Gallagher, *New Women in the Old West*, 12–13.
2. Edwards, Friefeld and Wingo, *Homesteading the Plains*, 136.
3. Edwards, Friefeld and Wingo, *Homesteading the Plains*, 134.
4. Knapp, "First Woman Homesteader."
5. Kelley, *Women of Nebraska*, 10.
6. Edwards, Friefeld, and Wingo, *Homesteading the Plains*, 140–42.
7. Naugle, Montag and Olson, *History of Nebraska*, 240–41.
8. Gallagher, *New Women in the Old West*, 71; Edwards, Friefeld and Wingo, *Homesteading the Plains*, 140.
9. Lock, "'As Independent as We Wished,'" 138–39.
10. Lock, "'As Independent as We Wished,'" 140–41.
11. "Two Blaine County Young Women Rather Run a Ranch Than a School," *Morning World-Herald* (Omaha, Nebraska), May 4, 1902.
12. "Two Blaine County Young Women."
13. Lock, "'As Independent as We Wished,'" 142.
14. Lock, "'As Independent as We Wished,'" 142.
15. Lock, "'As Independent as We Wished,'" 142.
16. "Two Blaine County Young Women."
17. "Two Blaine County Young Women."
18. Lock, "'As Independent as We Wished,'" 139, 147.
19. Lock, "'As Independent as We Wished,'" 143.

20. Lock, "'As Independent as We Wished,'" 146.
21. Lock, "'As Independent as We Wished,'" 143–44.
22. Lock, "'As Independent as We Wished,'" 144–45.
23. Lock, "'As Independent as We Wished,'" 147–48.
24. Lock, "'As Independent as We Wished,'" 148.
25. Lock, "'As Independent as We Wished,'" 149.

2. Crusaders: Anna Woodbey, Ada Bittenbender and Clara Colby

26. "Temperance Movement," Wikipedia, https://en.wikipedia.org.
27. Nebraska Commission on the Status of Women [hereafter Nebraska Commission], *Nebraska Women Through the Years*, 2; Bittenbender, History of WCTU in Nebraska.
28. Gallagher, *New Women in the Old West*, 41.
29. Hickman, "Thou Shalt Not Vote," 56; Nebraska Commission, *Nebraska Women Through the Years*, 22–23.
30. "Prohibition Party Candidates," History Nebraska, https://history. nebraska.gov; "Our Candidates," *Our Nation's Anchor* (Lincoln, Nebraska), July 20, 1895; Fletcher, "Notable African American Women."
31. Bittenbender, History of WCTU in Nebraska.
32. "Our Candidates."
33. Gaster, "Woodbey for Regent!"
34. Willard and Livermore, *Woman of the Century*, 87.
35. Willard and Livermore, *Woman of the Century*, 87; Hickman, "Thou Shalt Not Vote," 55.
36. Bloomberg, "'Striving for Equal Rights for All,'" 86–87; Nebraska Commission, *Nebraska Women Through the Years*, 24.
37. Stevens, *Dangerous Class*, 4–7.
38. Stevens, *Dangerous Class*, 9–10.
39. Kelley, *Women of Nebraska*, 20.
40. Nebraska Commission, *Nebraska Women Through the Years*, 24; Stevens, *Dangerous Class*, 9–14.
41. Bittenbender, History of WCTU in Nebraska.
42. Bittenbender, History of WCTU in Nebraska; Willard and Livermore, *Woman of the Century*, 87–88.
43. Willard and Livermore, *Woman of the Century*, 88; "Well Known Woman Dies," *Lincoln (NE) Journal Star*, December 15, 1925.
44. Stevens, *Dangerous Class*, 12.

45. Reeves, *Blue Book of Nebraska Women*, 21.
46. "Clara Bewick Colby," Wikipedia, https://en.wikipedia.org.
47. "Clara Bewick Colby," Wikipedia; Bloomberg, "'Striving for Equal Rights for All,'" 172–73, 175–76, 180–82.
48. Stevens, *Dangerous Class*, 18.
49. Wirth, *From Society Page to Front Page*, 37–38.
50. Reeves, *Blue Book of Nebraska Women*, 37–38.
51. Nebraska Commission, *Nebraska Women Through the Years*, 24.
52. Stevens, *Dangerous Class*, 31–25.
53. Stevens, *Dangerous Class*, 35.

3. Philanthropists: The Creighton Sisters, Anna Wilson and Sarah Joslyn

54. Wirth, *Women Who Built Omaha*, 20–21.
55. Wirth, *Women Who Built Omaha*, 19–21.
56. Wirth, *Women Who Built Omaha*, 22–23.
57. "Anna Wilson of Aristocratic Family," *Omaha (NE) Daily News*, November 6, 1911.
58. "Anna Wilson of Aristocratic Family"; Wirth, *Women Who Built Omaha*, 53–54.
59. Wirth, *Women Who Built Omaha*, 54.
60. "Anna Wilson of Aristocratic Family."
61. "Miss Anna Wilson Dies of Stroke of Paralysis," *Morning World-Herald* (Omaha, Nebraska), October 28, 1911.
62. Wirth, *Women Who Built Omaha*, 54.
63. Wirth, *Women Who Built Omaha*, 54; "Miss Anna Wilson Dies of Stroke of Paralysis."
64. "Opposed to Accepting Anna Wilson's Offer," *Omaha (NE) Daily News*, August 4, 1911.
65. Edwards, "There Is Also an Objection."
66. Edwards, "There is Also an Objection."
67. "City Takes Over the Anna Wilson Property," *Evening World-Herald* (Omaha, Nebraska), August 30, 1911.
68. "Miss Anna Wilson Dies of Stroke of Paralysis."
69. "Old People's Home to Get Two Residences," *Evening World-Herald* (Omaha, Nebraska), October 30, 1911.
70. "Charity Benefits by Anna Wilson's Will," *Morning World-Herald* (Omaha,

Nebraska), November 1, 1911.

71. "Miss Anna Wilson Dies of Stroke of Paralysis."

72. Wirth, *Women Who Built Omaha*, 53.

73. Mihelich, "Joslyns of Omaha," 2–3; Wirth, *Women Who Built Omaha*, 89.

74. Mihelich, "Joslyns of Omaha," 2–3.

75. Mihelich, "Joslyns of Omaha," 5.

76. "Gardens and Grounds," Joslyn Castle and Gardens, https://joslyncastle. com; Mihelich, "Joslyns of Omaha," 5–6.

77. Mihelich, "Joslyns of Omaha," 5–6.

78. Mihelich, "Joslyns of Omaha," 5.

79. Mihelich, "Joslyns of Omaha," 6–7.

80. Mihelich, "Joslyns of Omaha," 8–10; Wirth, *Women Who Built Omaha*, 90–92.

81. Mihelich, "Joslyns of Omaha," 9–10.

82. Mihelich, "Joslyns of Omaha," 8–9.

83. Wirth, *Women Who Built Omaha*, 90.

84. "Mrs. Joslyn to Build Memorial," *Morning World-Herald* (Omaha, Nebraska), May 6, 1928.

85. Wirth, *Women Who Built Omaha*, 91; Mihelich, "Joslyns of Omaha," 10–11.

86. Mihelich, "Joslyns of Omaha," 12.

87. Mihelich, "Joslyns of Omaha," 12.

4. Journalists: Elia Peattie and Harriet MacMurphy

88. Peattie, *Impertinences*, 17–18; Wirth, *From Society Page to Front Page*, 16–17, 20.

89. Wirth, *From Society Page to Front Page*, 21.

90. "Experience of Woman Editor," *Omaha (NE) Daily Bee*, February 21, 1907.

91. "Experience of Woman Editor."

92. Peattie, *Impertinences*, 17.

93. Wirth, *From Society Page to Front Page*, 23.

94. Peattie, *Impertinences*, 17; Wirth, *From Society Page to Front Page*, 19.

95. Peattie, *Impertinences*, 1–2; Reeves, *Blue Book of Nebraska Women*, 114.

96. Peattie, *Impertinences*, 3–5; Willard and Livermore, *Woman of the Century*; 562; Reeves, *Blue Book of Nebraska Women*, 114.

97. Willard and Livermore, *Woman of the Century*, 562; Peattie, *Impertinences*, 5.

98. Peattie, *Impertinences*, xv, 7–8, 11; Wirth, *From Society Page to Front Page*, 29.

99. Peattie, "In Defense of Her Own Sex."

100. Gallagher, *New Women in the Old West*, 53; Peattie, *Impertinences*, 12–13.

101. Peattie, *Impertinences*, 12–14; Reeves, *Blue Book of Nebraska Women*, 114–15.

102. Willard and Livermore, *Woman of the Century*, 562–63; Peattie, *Impertinences*, 8–10.

103. Peattie, *Impertinences*, 11–12.

104. Peattie, *Impertinences*, 10, 15.

105. Peattie, *Impertinences*, 15–16.

106. Peattie, *Impertinences*, 265; Wirth, *From Society Page to Front Page*, 31.

107. Nebraska Commission, *Nebraska Women Through the Years*, 39.

108. "Nebraska Newspaper Woman for Fifty Years," *Morning World-Herald* (Omaha, Nebraska), April 25, 1926.

109. "Nebraska Newspaper Woman for Fifty Years"; Kelley, *Women of Nebraska*, 22; Reeves, *Blue Book of Nebraska Women*, 98.

110. "Nebraska Newspaper Woman for Fifty Years."

111. "Nebraska Newspaper Woman for Fifty Years"; "Harriet MacMurphy Dies," *Omaha (NE) World-Herald*, July 20, 1932; Wirth, *From Society Page to Front Page*, 19.

112. "Nebraska Newspaper Woman for Fifty Years"; Reeves, *Blue Book of Nebraska Women*, 95–96.

113. Reeves, *Blue Book of Nebraska Women*, 96–97.

114. "Nebraska Newspaper Woman for Fifty Years."

115. Kelley, *Women of Nebraska*, 22; Reeves, *Blue Book of Nebraska Women*, 98; "Nebraska Newspaper Woman for Fifty Years."

116. Reeves, *Blue Book of Nebraska Women*, 99; "Nebraska Newspaper Woman for Fifty Years"; "Harriet MacMurphy Dies."

5. Civil Rights Activists: Ophelia Clenlans, Jessie Hale-Moss and Mildred Brown

117. "African American Settlers," Nebraska Studies, https://www.nebraskastudies.org.

118. "African American Settlers," Nebraska Studies; Naugle, Montag and Olson, *History of Nebraska*, 203.

119. Peattie, *Impertinences*, 58–62.

120. Peattie, *Impertinences*, 62–63, 103.

121. "Ophelia Clenlans," Wikipedia, https://www.wikipedia.org.

122. Fletcher, "Notable African American Women in Omaha History."

123. Peattie, *Impertinences*, 201.

124. Naugle, Montag and Olson, *History of Nebraska*, 309, 313; Forss, *Black*

Print with a White Carnation, 4–5.

125. Forss, *Black Print with a White Carnation*, 47.

126. Forss, *Black Print with a White Carnation*, 49.

127. Forss, *Black Print with a White Carnation*, 7; Fletcher, "Notable African American Women in Omaha History."

128. Fletcher, "Notable African American Women in Omaha History."

129. Fletcher, "Notable African American Women in Omaha History."

130. "Jessie Hale-Moss," *The Monitor* (Omaha, Nebraska), November 18, 1920.

131. Fletcher, "Notable African American Women in Omaha History"; "Jessie Hale-Moss."

132. Wirth, *From Society Page to Front Page*, 135–36.

133. Forss, *Black Print with a White Carnation*, 3–4, 34, 36.

134. Forss, *Black Print with a White Carnation*, 37–39.

135. Forss, *Black Print with a White Carnation*, 39–41; Wirth, *From Society Page to Front Page*, 138.

136. Forss, *Black Print with a White Carnation*, 43–44, 50–51; Wirth, *From Society Page to Front Page*, 138–39.

137. Wirth, *From Society Page to Front Page*, 137–38; Forss, *Black Print with a White Carnation*, 52.

138. Brown, "Publisher 'Ventured Forth.'"

139. Wirth, *From Society Page to Front Page*, 139; Forss, *Black Print with a White Carnation*, 61–62, 83, 94.

140. "Mildred Brown Dies; Omaha Star 'Era Ends,'" *Omaha (NE) World-Herald*, November 2, 1989.

141. "Mildred Brown Dies; Omaha Star 'Era Ends.'"

142. Forss, *Black Print with a White Carnation*, 8, 55.

143. Wirth, *Women Who Built Omaha*, 158; Forss, "Mildred Brown and the De Porres Club," 194.

144. Forss, "Mildred Brown and the De Porres Club," 194–95.

145. Forss, "Mildred Brown and the De Porres Club," 193, 197.

146. Forss, "Mildred Brown and the De Porres Club," 198–99.

147. Forss, "Mildred Brown and the De Porres Club," 200, 202.

148. Forss, "Mildred Brown and the De Porres Club," 197; Forss, *Black Print with a White Carnation*, 15, 136–37.

149. Forss, "Mildred Brown and the De Porres Club," 203; Forss, *Black Print with a White Carnation*, 125, 132–34.

150. Wirth, *From Society Page to Front Page*, 140; Forss, *Black Print with a White Carnation*, 18, 141, 144, 149, 150.

151. Fletcher, "Notable African American Women in Omaha History";

Wirth, *From Society Page to Front Page*, 137, 142.

152. Forss, *Black Print with a White Carnation*, 168–69; Brown, "Publisher 'Ventured Forth.'"

153. Forss, *Black Print with a White Carnation*, 2; Fletcher, "Notable African American Women in Omaha History;" Wirth, *From Society Page to Front Page*, 142.

6. Advocates for Native Americans: The LaFlesche Sisters

154. Starita, *Warrior of the People*, 3; Nebraska Commission, *Nebraska Women Through the Years*, 5.

155. Diffendal, "LaFlesche Sisters," 217–18; Starita, *Warrior of the People*, 10, 13–14.

156. Diffendal, "LaFlesche Sisters," 217–18; Starita, *Warrior of the People*, 14–16, 30.

157. Diffendal, "LaFlesche Sisters," 218; Wirth, *Women Who Built Omaha*, 29.

158. Diffendal, "LaFlesche Sisters," 218; Starita, *Warrior of the People*, 47–48, 61; Wirth, *Women Who Built Omaha*, 27–28.

159. Starita, *Warrior of the People*, 52; Wirth, *Women Who Built Omaha*, 29.

160. Starita, *Warrior of the People*, 53-54; Wirth, *Women Who Built Omaha*, 30.

161. Starita, *Warrior of the People*, 54; Wirth, *Women Who Built Omaha*, 30; Susette LaFleche letter to Thomas Tibbles, Thomas Henry Tibbles papers.

162. Diffendal, "LaFlesche Sisters," 219; Wirth, *Women Who Built Omaha*, 30–31; Starita, *Warrior of the People*, 56–57.

163. Tibbles, "Bright Eyes." This is from the first lecture Bright Eyes delivered in Boston.

164. Diffendal, "LaFlesche Sisters," 219–20.

165. Diffendal, "LaFlesche Sisters," 219; Wirth, *Women Who Built Omaha*, 32; Starita, *Warrior of the People*, 168–72.

166. Diffendal, "LaFlesche Sisters," 219; Nebraska Commission, *Nebraska Women Through the Years*, 6; Wirth, *Women Who Built Omaha*, 33.

167. Starita, *Warrior of the People*, 217–19; "Susette LaFlesche," Wikipedia, https://en.wikipedia.org.

168. Nebraska Commission, *Nebraska Women Through the Years*, 6; Diffendal, "LaFlesche Sisters," 221.

169. Diffendal, "LaFlesche Sisters," 220–21; "Alice Cunningham Fletcher," Wikipedia, https://en.wikipedia.org.

170. Diffendal, "The LaFlesche Sisters," 220; Starita, *A Warrior of the People*, 68–73; "Alice Cunningham Fletcher," Wikipedia.

171. Diffendal, "LaFlesche Sisters," 220–21.

172. Diffendal, "LaFlesche Sisters," 220–21; Nebraska Commission, *Nebraska Women Through the Years*, 6.

173. Diffendal, "LaFlesche Sisters," 221–22.

174. Starita, *Warrior of the People*, 197; Diffendal, "LaFlesche Sisters," 222.

175. Starita, *Warrior of the People*, 24, 28–30.

176. Starita, *Warrior of the People*, 57, 66–67, 84–86; Mathes, "Susan La Flesche Picotte," 503; Diffendal, "LaFlesche Sisters," 222.

177. Starita, *Warrior of the People*, 85–90.

178. Starita, *Warrior of the People*, 97–99.

179. Starita, *Warrior of the People*, 105.

180. Gallagher, *New Women in the Old West*, 116; Mathes, "Susan La Flesche Picotte," 504–6; Starita, *Warrior of the People*, 108–9, 114, 117, 120.

181. Starita, *Warrior of the People*, 145–47.

182. Mathes, "Susan La Flesche Picotte," 512; Diffendal, "LaFlesche Sisters," 222.

183. Starita, *Warrior of the People*, 159–61.

184. Starita, *Warrior of the People*, 162–64; Mathes, "Susan La Flesche Picotte," 513–16.

185. Starita, *Warrior of the People*, 161, 163–64, 178–79.

186. Starita, *Warrior of the People*, 186–89; Mathes, "Susan La Flesche Picotte," 516.

187. Diffendal, "LaFlesche Sisters," 221–23; Starita, *Warrior of the People*, 182, 195–96; Mathes, "Susan La Flesche Picotte," 518–19; Nebraska Commission, *Nebraska Women Through the Years*, 7.

188. Starita, *Warrior of the People*, 200–2; Mathes, "Susan La Flesche Picotte," 520.

189. Mathes, "Susan La Flesche Picotte," 521; Starita, *Warrior of the People*, 227–28.

190. Starita, *Warrior of the People*, 226, 237–38, 257; Mathes, "Susan La Flesche Picotte," 521.

191. Mathes, "Susan La Flesche Picotte," 519–20.

192. Starita, *Warrior of the People*, 210–11.

193. Starita, *Warrior of the People*, 212, 267.

194. Starita, *Warrior of the People*, 261–63, 267; Diffendal, "LaFlesche Sisters," 223.

195. "Presbyterian Hospital Opened with Appropriate Services," *Walthill (NE) Times*, January 10, 1913.

196. "Presbyterian Hospital Opened with Appropriate Services."

197. Starita, *Warrior of the People*, 198–99, 271–73; Mathes, "Susan La Flesche Picotte," 524.

198. Starita, *Warrior of the People*, 274.

199. Mathes, "Susan La Flesche Picotte," 525; "Susan LaFlesche Picotte Memorial Hospital," Explore Nebraska History, https://mynehistory.com; "Dr. Susan LaFlesche Picotte," Nebraska State Historical Society Foundation, https://www.nshsf.org.

7. Educator and Athlete: Louise Pound

200. Gallagher, *New Women in the Old West*, xx, 98.

201. Gallagher, *New Women in the Old West*, 52, 84.

202. Krohn, *Louise Pound*, 34, 40.

203. Kelley, *Women of Nebraska*, 38.

204. Krohn, *Louise Pound*, 9.

205. Krohn, *Louise Pound*, 19–20.

206. Krohn, *Louise Pound*, 5.

207. Krohn, *Louise Pound*, 21–22, 62, 83; Simpson, "Louise Pound."

208. Krohn, *Louise Pound*, 76–79; Cognard, "Louise Pound," 149.

209. Nebraska Commission, *Nebraska Women Through the Years*, 43; Krohn, *Louise Pound*, 115–16, 118, 125, 127, 162–65.

210. Krohn, *Louise Pound*, 51.

211. Krohn, *Louise Pound*, 32–33.

212. Krohn, *Louise Pound*, 42–43.

213. Krohn, *Louise Pound*, 52–53, 55.

214. Krohn, *Louise Pound*, 40, 86–86.

215. Krohn, *Louise Pound*, 3, 104, 106.

216. Krohn, *Louise Pound*, 87–88, 95–97; Simpson, "Louise Pound."

217. Simpson, "Louise Pound."

218. Krohn, *Louise Pound*, 5, 109, 149–53.

219. Krohn, *Louise Pound*, 5, 149, 153, 156, 189.

220. Krohn, *Louise Pound*, 123.

221. Kelley, *Women of Nebraska*, 38; Cognard, "Louise Pound," 150, Krohn, *Louise Pound*, 110, 134, 149, 171, 173.

222. Krohn, *Louise Pound*, 134; Cognard, "Louise Pound," 149.

223. Cognard, "Louise Pound," 150; Krohn, *Louise Pound*, 170; Simpson, "Louise Pound."

224. Krohn, *Louise Pound*, 129, 184, 193–94.

225. Krohn, *Louise Pound*, 132, 133.

226. Krohn, *Louise Pound*, 137, 139, 178–80.

227. Krohn, *Louise Pound*, 205.

228. Krohn, *Louise Pound*, 189, 228.

229. Krohn, *Louise Pound*, 208–9.

8. Great Plains Artist: Elizabeth Dolan

230. Stevens, "Elizabeth Honor Dolan," 175; Kennedy, "Nebraska Women Artists," 64, 73.

231. Willard and Livermore, *Woman of the Century*, 517; Kennedy, "Nebraska Women Artists," 65.

232. Kennedy, "Nebraska Women Artists," 65–66.

233. Kennedy, "Nebraska Women Artists," 66–67.

234. Kennedy, "Nebraska Women Artists," 67–68.

235. Stevens, "Elizabeth Honor Dolan," 175.

236. Mahoney, "Murals in Morrill Hall."

237. Kennedy, "Nebraska Women Artists," 74; Mahoney, "Murals in Morrill."

238. Mahoney, "Murals in Morrill"; Stevens, "Elizabeth Honor Dolan," 176; Kennedy, "Nebraska Women Artists," 74.

239. Mahoney, "Murals in Morrill Hall."

240. Mahoney, "Murals in Morrill Hall."

241. Stevens, "Elizabeth Honor Dolan," 178.

242. Stevens, "Elizabeth Honor Dolan," 176; Mahoney, "Murals in Morrill Hall."

243. Stevens, "Elizabeth Honor Dolan," 180; Kennedy, "Nebraska Women Artists," 74.

244. Stevens, "Elizabeth Honor Dolan," 179; Kennedy, "Nebraska Women Artists," 75–76.

245. Kennedy, "Nebraska Women Artists," 75; Stevens, "Elizabeth Honor Dolan," 179–80.

246. Stevens, "Elizabeth Honor Dolan," 180; Kelley, *Women of Nebraska*, 76; Kennedy, "Nebraska Women Artists," 75.

9. Writers: Willa Cather, Bess Streeter Aldrich and Mari Sandoz

247. Keene, *Willa Cather*, 2; Rosowski, "Willa Cather," 80–81.

248. Keene, *Willa Cather*, 6–7, 12–13.

249. Keene, *Willa Cather*, 14–15.

250. Keene, *Willa Cather*, 15–18.

251. Keene, *Willa Cather*, 21–22.

252. Keene, *Willa Cather*, 15–16, 23; Wirth, *From Society Page to Front Page*, 34–35; "Willa Cather Timeline," National Willa Cather Center, https://www.willacather.org.

253. Keene, *Willa Cather*, 23, 26–27; Nebraska Commission, *Nebraska Women Through the Years*, 43; Wirth, *From Society Page to Front Page*, 35.

254. Rosowski, "Willa Cather," 82, 85; Keene, *Willa Cather*, 57, 142–45; Kelley, *Women of Nebraska*, 40.

255. Keene, *Willa Cather*, 79–80.

256. Keene, *Willa Cather*, 144–45.

257. Keene, *Willa Cather*, 129; Kelley, *Women of Nebraska*, 40; "Willa Cather Statue Unveiled in National Statuary Hall of the U.S. Capitol," National Willa Cather Center, https://www.willacather.org.

258. Aldrich, "Story Behind *A Lantern*," 237, 239; Meier, "Bess Streeter Aldrich," 68–69.

259. Petersen, "Bess Streeter Aldrich," 139; Aldrich, "Story Behind *A Lantern*," 237; Meier, "Bess Streeter Aldrich," 70.

260. Meier, "Bess Streeter Aldrich," 70; Petersen, *Bess Streeter Aldrich*, 24.

261. Meier, "Bess Streeter Aldrich," 70–71; Petersen, "Bess Streeter Aldrich," 139.

262. Petersen, "Bess Streeter Aldrich," 139–40; Meier, "Bess Streeter Aldrich," 71–72.

263. Petersen, *Bess Streeter Aldrich*, 30, 37; Petersen, "Bess Streeter Aldrich," 139–40.

264. Meier, "Bess Streeter Aldrich," 79.

265. Meier, "Bess Streeter Aldrich," 73–74; Petersen, "Bess Streeter Aldrich," 141.

266. Petersen, *Bess Streeter Aldrich*, 97–98.

267. Petersen, *Bess Streeter Aldrich*, 64, 69; Petersen, "Bess Streeter Aldrich," 141.

268. Meier, "Bess Streeter Aldrich," 75; Petersen, *Bess Streeter Aldrich*, 50

269. Petersen, "Bess Streeter Aldrich," 141–42; Meier, "Bess Streeter Aldrich," 77.270. Petersen, "Bess Streeter Aldrich," 142; Meier, "Bess Streeter Aldrich," 82–83; Petersen, *Bess Streeter Aldrich*, 120–23.

271. Petersen, *Bess Streeter Aldrich*, 29, 115–16, 138, 177; Meier, "Bess Streeter Aldrich," 87–88, 90–91.

272. Meier, "Bess Streeter Aldrich," 87–88, 91–92.

273. Meier, "Bess Streeter Aldrich," 92.

274. Petersen, *Bess Streeter Aldrich*, 119.

275. Petersen, *Bess Streeter Aldrich*, 119–20.

276. Meier, "Bess Streeter Aldrich," 79, 83; Kelley, *Women of Nebraska*, 66.

277. Petersen, *Bess Streeter Aldrich*, 194, 197, 199–200.

278. Stauffer, "Mari Sandoz," 185; Wunder, "Some Notes on Mari Sandoz," 42; Stauffer, *Mari Sandoz*, 25.

279. Stauffer, "Mari Sandoz," 186; Stauffer, *Mari Sandoz*, 29; Greenwell, "Literary Apprenticeship of Mari Sandoz," 249; Wunder, "Some Notes on Mari Sandoz," 43.

280. Stauffer, *Mari Sandoz*, 30–33.

281. Stauffer, "Mari Sandoz," 186; Greenwell, "Literary Apprenticeship of Mari Sandoz," 251; Stauffer, *Mari Sandoz*, 41.

282. Stauffer, *Mari Sandoz*, 44–45, 49–50; Greenwell, "Literary Apprenticeship of Mari Sandoz," 252–53.

283. Wunder, "Some Notes on Mari Sandoz," 41; Stauffer, *Mari Sandoz*, 61; Greenwell, "Literary Apprenticeship of Mari Sandoz," 253.

284. Stauffer, *Mari Sandoz*, 68–69, 71; Greenwell, "Literary Apprenticeship of Mari Sandoz," 255.

285. Stauffer, *Mari Sandoz*, 69.

286. Stauffer, *Mari Sandoz*, 74.

287. Stauffer, *Mari Sandoz*, 84, 86–87; Greenwell, "Literary Apprenticeship of Mari Sandoz," 263–65.

288. Greenwell, "Literary Apprenticeship of Mari Sandoz," 265; Stauffer, *Mari Sandoz*, 94.

289. Greenwell, "Literary Apprenticeship of Mari Sandoz," 267; Stauffer, *Mari Sandoz*, 8, 97, 104–6, 111.

290. Stauffer, "Mari Sandoz," 189 90.

291. "A Review of the New Book," *Morning World-Herald* (Omaha, Nebraska), November 26, 1939; "An Interview with the Author," *Morning World-Herald* (Omaha, Nebraska), November 26, 1939.

292. Stauffer, "Mari Sandoz," 190–92; Stauffer, *Mari Sandoz*, 6.

293. Stauffer, *Mari Sandoz*, 159–64

294. Stauffer, *Mari Sandoz*, 189, 192–93.

295. Stauffer, "Mari Sandoz," 191; Stauffer, *Mari Sandoz*, 292–93.

296. Nebraska Commission, *Nebraska Women Through the Years*, 41; Stauffer, "Mari Sandoz," 185.

297. Stauffer, "Mari Sandoz," 184–85; Stauffer, *Mari Sandoz*, 198, 249, 255–56.

10. Entrepreneurs: Essie Davis and Rose Blumkin

298. McKelvie, *Sandhills Essie*, 12–14; Houston, "She Wouldn't Quit"; Kelley, *Women of Nebraska*, 70.

299. McKelvie, *Sandhills Essie*, 10–11.

300. McKelvie, *Sandhills Essie*, 16–17.

301. McKelvie *Sandhills Essie*, 22–23; Houston, "She Wouldn't Quit."

302. McKelvie, *Sandhills Essie*, 23–25; "Mrs. Davis, Career Woman, Builds Empire from Debts," *Lincoln (NE) Journal Star*, April 18, 1941.

303. "Mrs. Essie Davis, Only Woman Head of Credit Association, Loves Life in the Sand Hills," *Nebraska State Journal* (Lincoln, Nebraska), May 22, 1938; Kelley, *Women of Nebraska*, 70; "Mrs. Davis, Career Woman."

304. McKelvie, *Sandhills Essie*, 31–33; Houston, "She Wouldn't Quit;" "Mrs. Essie Davis, Only Woman Head."

305. McKelvie, *Sandhills Essie*, 25, 46–47; Houston, "She Wouldn't Quit."

306. McKelvie, *Sandhills Essie*, 40–42.

307. McKelvie, *Sandhills Essie*, 83–84; Houston, "She Wouldn't Quit"; "Mrs. Essie Davis, Only Woman Head."

308. Houston, "She Wouldn't Quit"; McKelvie, *Sandhills Essie*, 86–88.

309. McKelvie *Sandhills Essie*, 27–29.

310. McKelvie, *Sandhills Essie*, 67–68.

311. McKelvie, *Sandhills Essie*, 94–95.

312. Kelley, *Women of Nebraska*, 70; Houston, "She Wouldn't Quit."

313. Dorr, "Remembering Mrs. B"; Murray, "Cathy Hughes."

314. Wadler, "Omaha's Mrs. B."

315. Dorr, "Migrant"; Dorr, "Remembering Mrs. B"; Wadler, "Omaha's Mrs. B."

316. Dorr, "Remembering Mrs. B"; Wadler, "Omaha's Mrs. B"; Dorr, "Migrant."

317. Dorr, "Remembering Mrs. B"; Murray, "Cathy Hughes."

318. Dorr, "Migrant"; Dorr, "Remembering Mrs. B."

319. Dorr, "Remembering Mrs. B"; Dorr, "Migrant"; Wadler, "Omaha's Mrs. B"; Murray, "Cathy Hughes"; Wirth, *Women Who Built Omaha*, 112.

320. Murray, "Cathy Hughes"; Dorr, "Remembering Mrs. B."

321. Dorr, "Remembering Mrs. B"; Wirth, *Women Who Built Omaha*, 112.

322. Dorr, "Remembering Mrs. B"; Wirth, *Women Who Built Omaha*, 110.

323. Wadler, "Omaha's Mrs. B."

324. Dorr, "Remembering Mrs. B."

BIBLIOGRAPHY

Articles

Aldrich, Bess Streeter. "The Story Behind *A Lantern in Her Hand*." *Nebraska History* 56 (1975): 236–41.

Bloomberg, Kristin Mapel. "'Striving for Equal Rights for All': Woman Suffrage in Nebraska, 1855–1882." *Nebraska History* 90 (2009): 84–103.

Brown, Kathy. "Publisher 'Ventured Forth' to Long, Honor-Rich Career." *Omaha (NE) World-Herald*, May 27, 1984.

Cognard, Anne M. "Louise Pound: Renaissance Woman." In *Perspectives: Women in Nebraska History*, edited by Susan Pierce, 148–66. Nebraska Department of Education, 1984.

Diffendal, Anne P. "The LaFlesche Sisters: Susette, Rosalie, Marguerite, Lucy, Susan." In *Perspectives: Women in Nebraska History*, edited by Susan Pierce, 216–25. Nebraska Department of Education, 1984.

Dorr, Robert. "Migrant: Fruits of Labor Grow 'Only in America.'" *Omaha (NE) World-Herald*, September 28, 1977.

———. "Remembering Mrs. B," *Omaha (NE) World-Herald*, August 10, 1998.

Edwards, C.E. "There Is Also an Objection." *Omaha (NE) Daily News*, August 6, 1911.

Forss, Amy Helene. "Mildred Brown and the De Porres Club: Collective Activism in Omaha, Nebraska's, Near North Side, 1947–1960." *Nebraska History* 91 (2010): 190–205.

Greenwell, Scott L. "The Literary Apprenticeship of Mari Sandoz." *Nebraska History* 57 (1976): 248–72.

Hickman, Laura McKee. "Thou Shalt Not Vote: Anti-Suffrage in Nebraska, 1914–1920." *Nebraska History* 80 (1999): 55–65.

Houston, Robert. "She Wouldn't Quit." *Morning World-Herald* (Omaha, Nebraska), August 19, 1951.

Kennedy, Sharon L. "Nebraska Women Artists, 1880–1950." *Nebraska History* 88 (2007): 62–95.

Lock, William D. "'As Independent as We Wished': Elizabeth Scott & Alice Fish of Blaine County, Nebraska." *Nebraska History* 82 (2001): 138–51.

Mahoney, Eva. "Murals in Morrill Hall Bring Fame to Nebraska Woman." *Morning World-Herald* (Omaha, Nebraska), June 24, 1928.

Mathes, Valerie Sherer. "Susan La Flesche Picotte: Nebraska's Indian Physician, 1865–1915." *Nebraska History* 63 (1982): 502–30.

Meier, A. Mabel. "Bess Streeter Aldrich: A Literary Portrait." *Nebraska History* 50 (1969): 66–100.

Mihelich, Dennis N. "The Joslyns of Omaha: Opulence and Philanthropy." *Nebraska History* 83 (2002): 2–14.

Peattie, Elia. "In Defense of Her Own Sex." *Morning World-Herald* (Omaha, NE), December 1, 1895.

Petersen, Carol Miles. "Bess Streeter Aldrich: Celebrant of the Traditional Woman in Nebraska." In *Perspectives: Women in Nebraska History*, edited by Susan Pierce, 138–43. Nebraska Department of Education, 1984.

Rosowski, Susan J. "Willa Cather: Living History." In *Perspectives: Women in Nebraska History*, edited by Susan Pierce, 80–96. Nebraska Department of Education, 1984.

Simpson, Evelyn. "Louise Pound, Sports Champion." *Morning World-Herald* (Omaha, Nebraska), May 27, 1945.

Stauffer, Helen Winter. "Mari Sandoz, 1896–1966." In *Perspectives: Women in Nebraska History*, edited by Susan Pierce, 184–94. Nebraska Department of Education, 1984.

Stevens, Connie L. "Elizabeth Honor Dolan." In *Perspectives: Women in Nebraska History*, edited by Susan Pierce, 174–82. Nebraska Department of Education, 1984.

Wadler, Joyce. "Omaha's Mrs. B Tells Her Legendary Success Story." *Lincoln (NE) Journal Star*, June 5, 1984

Wunder, John R. "Some Notes on Mari Sandoz." *Prairie Schooner* 80, no. 4 (2006): 41–54.

Books

Edwards, Richard, Jacob K. Friefeld and Rebecca S. Wingo. *Homesteading the Plains: Toward a New History*. University of Nebraska Press, 2017.

Forss, Amy Helene. *Black Print with a White Carnation: Mildred Brown and the Omaha Star Newspaper, 1938–1989*. University of Nebraska Press, 2013.

Gallagher, Winifred. *New Women in the Old West: From Settlers to Suffragists, an Untold American Story*. Penguin, 2022.

Keene, Ann T. *Willa Cather*. Messner, 1994.

Kelley, Peggy A. Volzke. *Women of Nebraska Hall of Fame*. Nebraska International Women's Year Coalition, 1976.

Krohn, Marie. *Louise Pound: The 19th Century Iconoclast Who Forever Changed America's Views on Women, Academics, and Sports*. American Legacy Historical Press, 2008.

McKelvie, Martha. *Sandhills Essie*. Dorrance & Company, 1964.

Naugle, Ronald C., John J. Montag and James C. Olson. *History of Nebraska*. 4th ed. University of Nebraska Press, 2014.

Nebraska Commission on the Status of Women. *Nebraska Women Through the Years, 1867–1967*. Johnsen Publishing Company, 1967.

Peattie, Elia Wilkinson. *Impertinences: Selected Writings of Elia Peattie, a Journalist in the Gilded Age*. Edited by Susanne George Bloomfield. University of Nebraska Press, 2005.

Petersen, Carol Miles. *Bess Streeter Aldrich: The Dreams Are All Real*. University of Nebraska Press, 1995.

Reeves, Winona Evans. *The Blue Book of Nebraska Women: A History of Contemporary Women*. Missouri Printing and Publishing, 1916.

Starita, Joe. *A Warrior of the People: How Susan La Flesche Overcame Racial and Gender Inequality to Become America's First Indian Doctor*. St. Martin's Press, 2016.

Stauffer, Helen Winter. *Mari Sandoz: Story Catcher of the Plains*. University of Nebraska Press, 1982.

Stevens, Betty. *A Dangerous Class: A History of Suffrage in Nebraska and the League of Women Voters of Nebraska*. League of Women Voters of Nebraska Education Fund, 1995.

Willard, Frances, and Mary Ashton Rice Livermore. *A Woman of the Century; Fourteen Hundred-Seventy Biographical Sketches Accompanied by Portraits of Leading American Women in All Walks of Life*. Moulton, 1893.

Wirth, Eileen M. *From Society Page to Front Page: Nebraska Women in Journalism.* University of Nebraska Press, 2013.

———. *The Women Who Built Omaha: A Bold and Remarkable History.* University of Nebraska Press, 2022.

Websites

Fletcher, Adam F.C. "Notable African American Women in Omaha History." North Omaha History. https://northomahahistory.com.

Gaster, Patricia C. "Woodbey for Regent! When the Nebraska Prohibition Party Nominated a Black Woman in 1895." History Nebraska. February 2011. https://history.nebraska.gov.

Knapp, Fred. "First Woman Homesteader Offers Glimpse of Little-Known History." Nebraska Public Media, December 3, 2013. https://nebraskapublicmedia.org/en/news/news-articles/first-woman-homesteader-offers-glimpse-of-little-known-history/.

Murray, Robyn. "Cathy Hughes, One of Most Powerful Women in Broadcasting, among Nebraska's Influential Women." USA Today, August 13, 2020. https://www.usatoday.com.

Tibbles, Susette LaFlesche. "Bright Eyes—30 December 1880." Archives of Women's Political Communication. Iowa State University. https://awpc.cattcenter.iastate.edu.

Newspapers

Lincoln (NE) Journal Star
The Monitor (Omaha, NE)
Nebraska State Journal (Lincoln, NE)
Omaha (NE) Daily Bee

Omaha (NE) Daily News
Omaha (NE) World-Herald
Our Nation's Anchor (Lincoln, NE)
Walthill (NE) Times

Archives

Bittenbender, Ada C. History of WCTU in Nebraska, 21 October 1892, Woman's Christian Temperance Union (Neb.), History Nebraska, Lincoln, Nebraska.

Susette LaFlesche letter to Thomas Tibbles, 29 April 1879, Thomas Henry Tibbles papers, box 1, folder 4, National Museum of the American Indian Archive Center, Smithsonian Institution, Washington, D.C. https://www.si.edu.

ABOUT THE AUTHOR

Andrea is a writer of history—both real and fictional. Her main interest is the late nineteenth-century American West, especially outlaws and lawmen, women, American Indian history and the mythic West. While she hesitates to call herself an expert, she knows more than she needs to about Doc Holliday, the troubles in Tombstone, Billy the Kid and the Lincoln County War (just ask her family). She has a bachelor's degree in history and Great Plains studies from the University of Nebraska–Lincoln, a master's degree in public history from Arizona State University and a master's degree in library and information science from the University of Arizona. She has worked for the National Archives and Records Administration for over twenty years. She lives in Lincoln, Nebraska, with her husband, two daughters and four cats.

Visit us at
www.historypress.com